PARIS EXPRESS

PARIS EXPRESS

SIMPLE FOOD FROM THE CITY OF STYLE

LAURA CALDER

Photography by Ancuța Iordăchescu

HarperCollins*Publishers*Ltd

HarperCollins Publishers Ltd
2 Bloor Street East, 20th Floor
Toronto, Ontario, Canada
M4W 1A8

www.harpercollins.ca

Library and Archives Canada Cataloguing in
Publication information is available upon request.

Food styling by Patti Hetherington

ISBN 978-1-44342-020-4

Printed and bound in Canada

DWF 9 8 7 6 5 4 3 2 1

This book is dedicated with great admiration and affection
to my long-time Parisian friends,

The Mooneys
(Chris Mooney, Clara Young, Tybalt, Zola, and Sigovia).

Like nobody else, they've taught me over the years how Paris truly is a moveable feast,
and that its magic can be recreated anywhere if you put your mind to it.

Contents

INTRODUCTION

I must confess right up front that there's a bit of a double entendre to the title, *Paris Express*. Although this is indeed a collection of easy recipes that don't take hours to prepare, it's not remotely trying to be the next 15-minute cookbook. Rather, it's an attempt to capture the spirit of Paris dining and to transport there in a jiffy any home cook who's longing to get into a Paris state of mind—a place of breeziness, insouciance, whimsy, beauty, and delight . . . frankly, to a place where time slows down a bit. I've written this book for myself as much as for anyone else.

Allow me to backtrack. The truth of the matter is that I did, in fact, start in on this book thinking it would be a "fast French food" sort of deal. But as I went along, it struck me that it was all feeling a bit phony. I realized I don't actually know anyone in France who considers speed a priority when it comes to food. (Look how long those people are prepared to queue up just to buy a baguette!) Even when I asked Paris friends for quick and easy recipes, their idea of what "quick" might mean ranged from 15 minutes to three hours. Then it dawned on me: this is why Paris is my city! Somehow it manages to be a big, civilized metropolis and still feel like a carefree village brimming over with all the time and beauty in the world. No wonder it draws me like a magnet.

And so, I changed my tune. If this book was going to be true to my experience of cooking and eating in Paris, I couldn't with any conscience stand behind it cracking a whip. I'd make sure the recipes were quick and/or easy, but it would be unfair to make that the point, because, from a French perspective (and from mine), it isn't. After all, if you're happy where you are (for example, in the kitchen) and with what you're doing (for example, cooking dinner), then why would you be in a great hurry to get it all over with? Therein lies the greatest gulf between the attitude towards food in France and that in most other places.

I've been repeating myself for years, and I'll say it again: what really sets a place like Paris apart is not so much *what* people eat as it is their approach to eating in general. Dining in Paris, indeed anywhere in France, truly is a cultural phenomenon. People understand how eating well every day is key to living a good life. They are no more likely to run about town stark naked on the pretext that they didn't have time to get dressed in the morning than they are not to dine properly because the day had got away on them. They simply do it. (And by "they" I mean virtually everyone, not just a handful of "foodies.") Commonly, in fact, they'll dine for hours on end. This is their idea of a good time, of life as it should be lived!

This attitude towards eating is, of course, all part of something greater, what the French call *l'art de vivre*, the art of living, which is practically in their DNA. If they fix their hair before heading out to the dry cleaner's, it's not because they're vain; it's because they consider it a social responsibility to make themselves respectfully presentable to all those other people out in the world who are going to have to look at them. If they bother with their pleases and thank yous more than most of the rest of us, this is not excessive formality, but rather a practice considered essential to the good health of the soul, not to mention the essential grease that keeps the wheels of society turning. That same motivation is behind the French insistence on eating well and in style. And, incidentally, it's not that they have more time for this business than the rest of us; they *make* the time because, to them, these things matter.

It's not everywhere in the world where such "niceties" are considered, in fact, priorities. For those of us elsewhere, it can take some determination and extra effort to uphold such standards. But it's worth it because it makes the world a better place, it makes life more interesting to live, and it makes us happier, better-functioning people.

And so, in the end, this has not turned out to be the book about speed that it was initially intended to be. Instead, what it sets out to encourage—or one might say "to express"—is a way of creating for ourselves, however much we fight the clock, a richer life around the table, which inevitably ripples out into the wider world.

A NOTE *about the* RECIPES

I have the great good luck when I'm in Paris of being surrounded by an unusually high number of excellent home cooks. I more or less live and breathe dinner parties when I'm there, and I find the level of creativity around me unrivalled. There's probably a notion in the outside world that in France people spend all their livelong days cooking and then eating coq au vin and boeuf bourguignon and îles flottantes. Those classics are certainly still very much in circulation, but the modern palate is curious: more and more new flavours from around the world are making their way onto the plate, and Parisian cooking has become increasingly playful, light, and inspired since my early days in the city. Besides, the home cooks whose company I keep are adventurous and experimental sorts.

This will explain why some recipes in this book may not strike you as being overwhelmingly French. A few are more reflective of the non-French influences in the city, which in their own way make Parisian cuisine unique. Obviously North African flavours are ubiquitous in France. Japanese food is much more prevalent than Chinese in Paris. Scandinavian flavours are a trend at the time of writing. Influences such as these, layered on top of the firm foundations of French cooking, make for a lively food scene, and that's the one I hope I have captured—what's alive and thriving right now, not something ripped from a history book.

The recipes in *Paris Express* were all collected in Paris, mostly made for me by friends and relished *in situ*. Whenever I make them, I'm taken right back to that city and to the good times I've had cooking and eating there. Whether you've visited Paris yourself or merely dreamed of going, I hope these recipes will have the same positive teleporting effect on you, and inspire simple, spontaneous Parisian-style feasts in happy company.

FIRST C

O U R S E S

FIRST COURSES

Chilled Cucumber and Avocado Soup with Chive Flowers **9**

Chilled Yellow Pepper Soup **10**

Asparagus Soup with Orange-Parsley Toasted Bread Flakes **14**

Lentil and Chestnut Soup with Toasted Hazelnuts and Cream **15**

Pumpkin and Carrot Soup with Green Peppercorns **18**

Watercress Soup **19**

Asparagus, Pea, and Fava Salad **21**

Young Lettuce with Chives and Cream **24**

White Peach and Yellow Tomato Salad **27**

Mixed Leaves with Truffle Oil Dressing **28**

Mâche with Almonds, Olives, and Orange Dressing **29**

Fig and Arugula Salad with Prosciutto **33**

Butter Lettuce with Flowers and Foie Gras **35**

Endive and Frisée Salad with Blue Cheese and Walnuts **36**

Grated Carrot Salad **37**

Fennel and Radicchio Salad with Date and Anchovy Dressing **41**

Warm Broccoli Salad **42**

Easy Artichokes with "Bastard Sauce" **43**

Mushrooms en Papillote **44**

White Asparagus with Almond Cream **47**

Linguine with Cherry Tomato Sauce **50**

Bow Ties with Mushrooms and Basil **51**

Swiss Chard "Risotto" **53**

Buckwheat Noodles with Caviar **56**

Grilled Prawns and Radicchio with Bagna Cauda **57**

Glam Clams **59**

Easy Oysters **60**

Mussels in Saffron Cream **65**

Sashimi Mio **66**

Soused Herring Sandwiches **67**

Minty Sardine Tartines **68**

Chicken Liver Pâté That I Actually Want to Eat **70**

Lard Pastry **71**

Mushroom Tart with Tarragon and Smoked Gouda **72**

Red Onion Tart **75**

CHILLED CUCUMBER *and* AVOCADO SOUP *with* CHIVE FLOWERS

I'm hard pressed to come up with a speedier first course than this one. This beautiful and refreshing summer soup should be served in small portions, as it's quite rich. Having said that, if you want to make it more substantial still for a main-course lunch, a spoonful of well-seasoned crabmeat on top of each portion won't go amiss.

1-1/2 English cucumbers, peeled and cut into chunks
1 avocado, peeled, pitted, and cut into chunks
Juice of 1 lemon
1-1/2 cups (375 mL) vegetable or chicken stock
1/2 teaspoon ground cumin
1 to 2 garlic cloves, crushed
1/4 cup (60 mL) heavy cream
Salt and pepper
High-quality olive oil, for garnish
2 to 3 chive blossoms, for garnish

Combine the cucumber chunks, avocado, and lemon juice. Pour over the stock, add the cumin and garlic, and purée.

Pour the mixture into a bowl or jug. Stir in the cream and season with salt and pepper. Cover and chill until serving.

To serve, pour or ladle into bowls. Drizzle with olive oil. Pull apart the chive blossoms and scatter a few purple petals over each bowl.

MAKES: 8 SERVINGS

CHILLED YELLOW PEPPER SOUP

A light, cold soup with happy colour and appealing heat to please the tongue. I like to put a garnish of very small fried croutons on top with maybe a bit of diced tomato, slivered shallot, and fresh coriander. Crab and coriander would be good another day.

3 yellow peppers, coarsely chopped
1 large yellow tomato
1/4 white onion (or 1 shallot), coarsely chopped
1 small garlic clove
2 tablespoons olive oil
1 teaspoon red wine vinegar
Salt and black pepper
Pinch cayenne pepper or piment d'Espelette

Combine all the ingredients and purée. Chill. Serve with an imaginative garnish (see headnote.)

MAKES: 6 SERVINGS

Making Menus

I adore dreaming up menus. Indeed, it is a task (wrong word . . . "activity"? "undertaking"? "obsession"? "calling"?) that I relish in the way that others might do deciding what to wear to parties. Perhaps the world could be divided into these two categories, because I never know what I'm going to wear anywhere until whatever it is I'm wearing is actually on my back. Not good, I suppose, but my attention always seems to be elsewhere. Planning a menu, on the other hand, can keep me awake nights!

Dinner parties in Paris tend to be spontaneous occasions. They may be inspired quite suddenly by someone announcing, "Hear ye, hear ye, I just got my hands on a suckling pig!" Another time, a kooky desire to create a little fun out of nothing will be the instigator. (I'm thinking of a "dinner party" once during the Christmas holidays when someone, fed up with all the to-doings, instructed everyone to show up wearing pyjamas and served pancakes, bacon, and beans. Take that, Paris!) A dinner can come about by a phone call made as late as 6 p.m. on a weeknight: "What are you doing?" "Nothing." "Me neither. Come over—we'll make something." And then there's just getting home late and saying to whoever else is in the house, "What do you feel like?"

Obviously, if we've got our hands on a few truffles from Alba and have called choice friends to come share them, or if someone in our circle has a birthday coming up ending in *0*, we're going to undertake more in-depth, careful, and advanced menu planning than if we're standing in front of a nearly-empty refrigerator on a Tuesday night trying desperately to conjure up something inspired that involves two eggs, half a cucumber, and a tub of coconut yogurt. (Good luck with that!) But the point is that no matter how spur of the moment deciding what we're going to eat may be, and no matter how apparently inconsequential, we still do make a plan. Presumably one that will feed our physical and emotional needs in the most satisfying way possible and bring us the greatest pleasure in that particular instant.

I'd be interested to see, if I could ever get organized enough to the keep this sort of diary, what a full year of my own dinner menus would look like. I confess, I'd like a peek into other people's logs, too. Just imagine the range! Consider what hints about their lives might inadvertently be revealed!

April 21st: *poule au pot*, chocolate pudding (Status quo.)
January 1st: caviar and champagne, beef consommé, lobster à l'Armoricaine, gâteau Saint Honoré (Hmm, good fiscal year behind them, would seem …)
October 13th: Pizza Pizza
October 14th: cereal
October 15th: tinned beans (What on *earth* is going on?!)
October 17th: 8-course tasting menu at The Bristol (Oh, I guess they must have made up.)

You see what I mean? It may not be immediately apparent on the surface, but menus, whether quickly flung together, calculated like a military coup, or simply imposed upon us because we're in the right or wrong place at the right or wrong time, are actually little stories. They capture the tale of a moment and seal the memory like a licked envelope. If we open them up later and read between the lines, we'll be able to read, "I was there … here's how it was … this is what happened …"

ASPARAGUS SOUP *with* ORANGE-PARSLEY TOASTED BREAD FLAKES

I used to think asparagus soup was a waste, because for some reason I felt the spears were too precious to "reduce" to purée. But when asparagus is in season and you find yourself eating it night after night, you start wanting to see it in a new form, which is how I came to try it as soup, as so many wise cooks have done before me. Well, it is not diminishing at all! In fact, it's now one of my favourite ways to eat asparagus. I love dipping my spoon into the pool of pale green loveliness and then letting the soup's surprising, sprightly flavour fill my mouth.

For the soup

2 tablespoons butter

1 onion, sliced

2 pounds (900 g) asparagus, trimmed and
   coarsely chopped

3 cups (750 mL) chicken stock

1/2 cup (125 mL) heavy cream

Salt and black pepper

Pinch cayenne pepper (optional)

A squeeze of lemon juice (optional)

For the garnish

1 cup (60 g) fresh flaky bread crumbs
   (p. 207)

2 tablespoons butter, melted

A few handfuls of finely chopped
   fresh parsley

Zest of 1 orange

Pinch salt

For the soup, melt the butter in a large saucepan and gently fry the onion until softened, about 5 minutes. Add the asparagus, pour over the stock, and simmer until tender, 10 to 15 minutes. Purée with the cream. Season with salt, black pepper, and cayenne and lemon juice (if using). Reheat before serving.

For the garnish, preheat the oven to 400°F (200°C). Toss the crumbs with the melted butter and spread on a baking sheet. Toast in the oven until golden, 3 to 5 minutes. Tilt into a small serving bowl and stir through the parsley and orange zest. Sprinkle in a little salt.

To serve, ladle the warm soup into warm bowls. Pass the garnish separately with a spoon for scattering over the soup.

MAKES: 6 TO 8 SERVINGS

LENTIL *and* CHESTNUT SOUP
with TOASTED HAZELNUTS *and* CREAM

This soup is elegant and earthy all at once, making a nourishing lunch on an autumn day or a soothing starter when you've planned a light main course.

2 tablespoons olive oil

1 large onion, minced

3 garlic cloves, crushed

2 bay leaves

1 sprig fresh thyme

1 cup (200 g) du Puy lentils

11 ounces (300 g) jarred or vacuum-packed peeled chestnuts

6 cups (1.5 L) water or chicken or mushroom stock

Salt and pepper

Heavy cream, for garnish

A handful of toasted hazelnuts or walnuts, chopped, for garnish

Heat the oil in a soup pot and gently fry the onion until soft, about 8 minutes. Add the garlic and cook, stirring, for 1 minute. Drop in the bay leaves and thyme, spill in the lentils and chestnuts, and pour in the water or stock. Bring to a simmer and cook until the lentils and chestnuts are tender, about 30 minutes.

Remove the bay leaves and the thyme sprig. Purée the soup. Season with salt and pepper. Reheat and ladle into warm bowls, giving each serving a swirl of cream and a scattering of chopped nuts.

MAKES: 8 SERVINGS

PUMPKIN *and* CARROT SOUP *with* GREEN PEPPERCORNS

This is one of the most stunning versions of pumpkin soup I've ever tasted, thanks to the mysterious depth of flavour added by the green peppercorns. In France I use potiron pumpkin. Elsewhere, you will have excellent results with a small sugar pumpkin or butternut or with buttercup squash.

1/4 cup (55 g) butter
3 pounds (1.35 kg) pumpkin or squash, peeled, seeded, and chopped
11 ounces (300 g) carrots (about 2 large), peeled and chopped
1 bay leaf
1 tablespoon green peppercorns in brine, drained
Salt
4 cups (1 L) chicken stock, more if needed

Melt the butter in a soup pot over low heat. Add the pumpkin, carrots, bay leaf, and peppercorns. Season lightly with salt.

Pour over the stock, and simmer until the vegetables are tender, about 30 minutes. Purée the soup, in batches if necessary, adding a little more stock if the soup is too thick. Taste and adjust the seasonings. Reheat the soup and serve in warm bowls.

MAKES: 6 SERVINGS

WATERCRESS SOUP

This soup is lovely in all seasons, but most particularly as a first course in winter when we crave salad greens but get goosebumps at the very thought of eating anything chilly. You'll find this equally good made with lettuce and, either way, despite what I just said, delicious cold. Parmesan curls or a crumbling of blue cheese make a nice garnish. You could also, if you have some time, try the crêpe cracker idea on p. 213.

1 tablespoon olive oil
2 tablespoons butter
2 onions, chopped
1 large potato, peeled and sliced
1 pound (450 g) watercress
4 cups (1 L) water or chicken stock
1/4 cup (60 mL) heavy cream
Salt and pepper
A squeeze of lemon juice (optional)

Heat the oil and butter in a soup pot and gently fry the onions until translucent, about 8 minutes. Stir in the potato and watercress. Pour in the water or stock, bring to a boil, then reduce heat and simmer until the watercress is wilted and the potatoes are tender, about 10 minutes.

Purée the soup, then strain through a sieve, pressing on the solids. Return the smooth soup to the pot. Stir in the cream. Season with salt, pepper, and lemon juice if you like. Reheat before serving.

MAKES: 4 TO 6 SERVINGS

ASPARAGUS, PEA, *and* FAVA SALAD

Imagine a bowlful of spring, because that's what you have here: fresh peas, crunchy asparagus, buttery favas, briny green olives, a few threads of green from new shoots, and peppery arugula. It is utterly delightful to eat, and excellent before something like a creamy chicken dish. I have read that soaking sliced asparagus in ice-cold water for 15 minutes, then draining and patting it dry will keep it ultra-crisp in a salad, but I admit I've never bothered. If you like, serve with lightly toasted slices of baguette rubbed with a split garlic clove and drizzled with olive oil. You might even smear them with a bit of fresh chèvre. Leftovers of the salad remain good the next day.

7 ounces (200 g) fat green asparagus, trimmed

4 ounces (110 g) shelled fava beans

4 ounces (110 g) freshly shelled green peas

4 to 6 small radishes, very thinly sliced

4 ounces (110 g) sliced green olives

A handful of arugula

A handful of pea shoots, halved if very long

Zest of 1 lemon

2 to 3 tablespoons excellent olive oil

A squeeze of lemon juice

Salt and pepper

A handful of lightly toasted pine nuts

Parmesan cheese, for garnish

Slice the asparagus very thinly. Place in a large bowl with the favas, peas, radishes, olives, arugula, pea shoots, and lemon zest.

Pour over just enough olive oil to lightly coat the vegetables. Season with lemon juice, salt, and pepper. Toss to coat. Scatter over the pine nuts and shave over Parmesan cheese. Serve.

MAKES: 4 SERVINGS

Picnic on a Platter

Here's a clever way to feed unexpected drop-in friends with a bit of flourish: the French call it an *assiette de crudités*, and it's perfect for a light lunch or *apéro-dinatoire* (the term for an apéritif party that's intended to replace dinner). You'll need a nice big platter to start with, and upon it you artfully arrange things like julienned carrots, cooked green beans, halved boiled eggs, sliced cucumber and avocado, some curls of ham, possibly some marinated artichokes or boiled baby potatoes, a heap of tiny radishes . . . Whatever you've got around, you simply arrange all together on the platter to look as jewel-boxy as possible. Serve pots of vinaigrette and mayonnaise on the side, and let people help themselves. All you need to round out the feast are a few baguettes, perhaps a doorstop of Roquefort, and a bottle or two of chilled rosé.

YOUNG LETTUCE *with* CHIVES *and* CREAM

I remember Elizabeth David writing a thousand years ago about a dressing for lettuce consisting of little more than melted butter, a scrape of crushed garlic, and a squeeze of lemon. I've never actually tried it, which is odd considering how the concept so etched itself in my memory in youth. The dressing below, which is really nothing but a subtle veil of cream, brought E. D.'s recipe back to mind. It's *un petit rien* of a recipe, but worth knowing about because there are times when a creamy dressing is desirable, but without the heavy-handedness associated with bottled varieties. Some might like a dash of red wine vinegar or a squeeze of lemon juice here, but generally I find it unnecessary.

6 handfuls of buttery green lettuce leaves (about 8 ounces/225 g)
A few tablespoons of heavy cream
A generous handful of chopped fresh chives
Fleur de sel and freshly ground pepper

At the very last minute before serving, toss together all the ingredients. Serve.

MAKES: 6 SERVINGS

WHITE PEACH *and* YELLOW TOMATO SALAD

This glorious summer salad makes a nice change from tomatoes and mozzarella. It's essential that the tomatoes and peaches be of the highest quality and perfectly ripe. The olive oil, too, should be top-notch.

1-1/2 pounds (675 g) ripe peaches (about 4 medium), preferably white
1-1/2 pounds (675 g) ripe summer tomatoes (about 4 medium), preferably yellow
3 tablespoons olive oil of exceptional quality
Sel de Guérande or other fleur de sel
Freshly ground pepper
A few drops of balsamic vinegar (optional)
A few handfuls of shredded fresh basil

Bring a large pot of water to a boil. Score an X in the bottom of each peach, then plunge them into the water for 10 seconds. Drain and shock in ice-cold water. Peel, pit, and cut into wedges. Transfer to a large bowl. Cut the tomatoes into wedges the same size as the peaches; add to the peaches.

Toss the fruit with the olive oil and season with salt and pepper. Spill onto a serving platter. Drizzle on a little vinegar if you wish, scatter over the basil, and serve.

MAKES: 6 SERVINGS

MIXED LEAVES *with* TRUFFLE OIL DRESSING

I love the lingering taste of a good-quality truffle oil, which is why I tend to serve this salad not as a first course but rather, French style, before or with cheese before dessert. Sometimes I add half a fennel bulb, thinly shaved, along with the coarsely chopped fronds and a bit of lemon zest. (Without the fennel, the zest would be too overpowering, so don't be tempted.) The range of truffle oils is so vast (and note that some "truffle oil" is really just scented olive oil, in which case you could simply use that), you really must rely on your palate to adjust the final result, adding more truffle if you want it, more acid if it's needed, and so on. But the basic premise is this:

2 teaspoons Champagne vinegar

1 teaspoon Dijon mustard, preferably, but not necessarily, truffle scented

1/4 cup (60 mL) light olive or grapeseed oil

Truffle oil

A squeeze of lemon juice

Salt and pepper

6 good handfuls of mixed greens (about 9 ounces/250 g)

A handful or two of grated Parmesan cheese

A handful or two of coarsely chopped lightly toasted hazelnuts

In a salad bowl, whisk together the vinegar and mustard, then whisk in the olive oil in a thin stream until emulsified. Whisk in truffle oil and lemon juice to taste. Season with salt and pepper. Add the greens, Parmesan cheese, and nuts. Toss to coat, and serve immediately.

MAKES: 6 SERVINGS

MÂCHE *with* ALMONDS, OLIVES, *and* ORANGE DRESSING

A friend once served me a trio of orange slices liberally scattered with chopped black olives. It's a Mediterranean concoction that I can highly recommend. The delight of squirty orange against dense, briny black came as a surprise, which is why I've used the combination here to add excitement to a lamb's lettuce salad. Serve alone or with a selection of cheeses.

2 oranges
1/2 teaspoon Dijon mustard
1/4 cup (60 mL) excellent olive oil
Salt and pepper
4 ounces (110 g) mâche
1/4 cup (25 g) slivered almonds, lightly toasted
1/4 cup (25 g) chopped pitted black olives

Finely grate a teaspoon of zest from 1 orange and put it in a small bowl. Now juice both oranges. In a small saucepan, boil the juice until reduced to about 2 tablespoons.

Stir the mustard into the zest, then stir in the reduced juice. Whisk in the olive oil in a thin stream until emulsified. Season with salt and pepper.

Just before serving, toss the dressing with the greens, almonds, and olives.

MAKES: 6 SERVINGS

As Clean as the Air You Breathe

The trouble with commercial cleaning products is that as soon as you remove a lid, it's like being trapped in the back of a taxi with one of those suffocating cardboard "air fresheners" waving about from the rear-view mirror. Ugh. So I don't buy them. Dishwashing liquid is an exception, but otherwise, I'm a baking-soda-and-vinegar kind of girl. Window cleaner = a squirt bottle of vinegar and water and a crumpled-up sheet of newspaper. Sink scrubber = baking soda and a sponge. Floors = vinegar water again. Cutting boards = soap and water, vinegar to disinfect, and, periodically, an oil rub. Copper pot polish = salt, flour, lemon juice, and a soft cloth. I am infuriatingly self-righteous about all this, I know, but it does save a fortune, reduces clutter like you wouldn't believe, and keeps the kitchen toxin-free, which, one never knows, may well add a day or two to one's life. The other thing you should always have in the house is a cake of *savon de Marseille*. It's very good for getting stains out of things and for hand-washing clothes when you have to.

FIG *and* ARUGULA SALAD
with PROSCIUTTO

Splendour on a platter, this five-minute deal looks and tastes of late-summer bounty. Top-quality ingredients are key: figs ripe but firm, chèvre creamy fresh, arugula peppery, mâche nutty, and the prosciutto sliced by your butcher cigarette-paper thin. Balsamic glaze is available in most supermarkets, but if you can't find it, make your own by boiling inexpensive balsamic vinegar in a saucepan until it is syrupy, sweet, and rich—1 cup (250 mL) vinegar boiled for about 10 minutes should yield 1/3 cup (75 mL) glaze with the texture of light honey.

4 handfuls of mixed arugula and mâche

About 3 tablespoons olive oil

2 tablespoons balsamic glaze

Salt and pepper

8 fresh black figs, cut into quarters lengthwise

12 ultra-thin slices prosciutto or similar cured ham, cut into strands

6 ounces (170 g) very fresh high-quality chèvre, in pinches

2 handfuls of lightly toasted pine nuts

Toss 3 handfuls of the arugula and mâche with just enough olive oil and a drizzle of balsamic glaze to coat it lightly, then scatter it over a platter. Season with salt and pepper. Arrange the fig quarters on top, strew the ham and chèvre over top, followed by the remaining arugula and mâche leaves and the pine nuts. With a light hand, drizzle a little more olive oil and glaze on top. Serve.

MAKES: 6 SERVINGS

BUTTER LETTUCE *with* FLOWERS *and* FOIE GRAS

This is a spectacular salad for special occasions, extremely pretty, to-die-for delicious . . . and staggeringly expensive. It is worth every penny, though.

Leaves from 2 heads butter lettuce, trimmed
A good handful of fresh tarragon leaves, chopped
A handful of fresh flat-leaf parsley leaves, coarsely chopped
A small handful of fresh chives, chopped
1 garlic clove, crushed
1 tablespoon Champagne vinegar or lemon juice
1 teaspoon Dijon mustard
1/4 cup (60 mL) olive oil
Salt and pepper
4 ounces (110 g) foie gras, frozen
A few handfuls of edible flower petals (about 2 ounces/55 g)
A few handfuls of pine nuts (about 1/3 cup/75 mL), lightly toasted

Tear the lettuce leaves a bit to make them fork friendly and put them in a large bowl with all the herbs.

In a small bowl, whisk together the garlic, vinegar, and mustard, then whisk in the olive oil in a thin stream until emulsified. Season with salt and pepper.

Using a sharp knife, shave the foie gras over the salad. Scatter with the flowers and pine nuts. Toss with the dressing and serve immediately.

MAKES: 8 SERVINGS

ENDIVE *and* FRISÉE SALAD *with* BLUE CHEESE *and* WALNUTS

A classic recipe is usually best left untampered-with, although here you could replace the blue cheese with sections of orange. In the latter case, it's the sweetness that foils the slightly bitter greens; in the former it's the salt and creaminess of the cheese.

5 ounces (140 g) white frisée, torn

3 endives (about 6 ounces/170 g each), halved and cored

2 teaspoons red wine vinegar

1/2 teaspoon Dijon mustard

2 tablespoons olive oil

Salt and pepper

4 ounces (110 g) blue cheese

1/2 ounce (15 g) walnuts, toasted and coarsely chopped

Put the frisée and endives in a large salad bowl. In a small bowl, whisk together the vinegar and mustard, then whisk in the olive oil in a thin stream until emulsified. Season with salt and pepper. Toss with the greens, then crumble over the cheese and scatter over the nuts. Serve.

MAKES: 4 SERVINGS

GRATED CARROT SALAD

It may sound odd to sit down to a plate of grated carrots, but try *carottes râpées*, as the French call it, and you'll see why it's such a hit. Tasty, organic carrots are a must, but from there the variations are endless. I've tried this with various herbs, with nuts or seeds, and with different oils and vinegars, but the version below—minimalist though it is—is the one I make most often. With a boiled egg on the side, you have lunch.

4 cups (225 g) grated carrots
2 to 3 generous handfuls of chopped fresh parsley
1/4 cup (60 mL) olive oil
A squeeze or two of lemon juice
A squirt of soy sauce
Salt and pepper

Toss the carrots in a roomy bowl with the parsley and olive oil. Season with lemon juice, soy sauce, salt, and pepper. Toss again and serve.

MAKES: 6 SERVINGS

Shop Like a Parisian

It can be a tricky business in some places to grocery shop like a Parisian, because here's how they do it: they sense dinner approaching, wonder what they'd like, then grab a basket, hop down the street, load up on ingredients, and come home and cook them. On market day, they may go out with plans less firm, intending simply to snap up the seasonal best and figure out what to do with it later. What they don't do is drive to a supermarket the size of a hockey arena and load up a cart the size of a Zamboni with two weeks' worth of supplies. I know what it's like to be living in a situation where the latter is a fact of life, but almost everywhere there are at least a few places with soul to supplement with. Increasingly, there are farmers' markets to visit on the weekends. There are plenty of ethnic food shops that have interesting things on offer. Specialists in meats and eggs and cheeses and spices and oils are dotted here and there. You just have to sniff them out, and even if they're not places you can visit every day, at least once a week if you can, get to a place that has some spirit and is on a human scale—and feel a few inches closer to Paris.

FENNEL *and* RADICCHIO SALAD *with* DATE *and* ANCHOVY DRESSING

This is one of the most arresting things I've ever eaten: bitter leaves and fragrant fennel juggling a dressing of sweet dates, heady garlic, salty anchovies, and fresh citrus. If you're making the dressing by hand, and especially if your dates are slightly on the dry side, chop the dates, then press them under your hand, before chopping again and flattening with the side of your knife. Ditto the anchovies. The dressing will be pasty, and you'll need to toss the salad gently with your hands so that the leaves are thoroughly coated.

1/2 large fennel bulb, cored and very thinly sliced crosswise

Leaves from 1 small radicchio, hard stems removed, torn in half

2 plump Medjool dates, pitted and coarsely chopped

6 anchovies, rinsed and coarsely chopped

1 garlic clove, crushed

1 teaspoon sherry vinegar

1/3 cup (75 mL) olive oil

Salt and pepper

A squeeze of lemon juice

Zest of 1/2 lemon

Zest of 1/2 orange

Parmesan cheese, for garnish

Put the fennel and radicchio in a bowl large enough for easy tossing.

Put the dates, anchovies, garlic, vinegar, and olive oil in a blender and whiz to a thin paste. Season with salt, pepper, and lemon juice.

Add the dressing to the fennel and radicchio. Add the lemon and orange zests, then toss gently with your hands to coat. Transfer to a serving dish and scatter over very, very thin curls of Parmesan cheese. Grind over a little more pepper, and serve.

MAKES: 4 SERVINGS

WARM BROCCOLI SALAD

Broccoli is a vegetable that often needs a little help. In this salad, the head is grated to confetti, then the stem is shaved into pale, crisp ribbons, which get tossed into a tangle along with a few handfuls of peppery, jagged-edged arugula and heady quantities of mint. The sautéed onion gives depth and warmth to the dish, while the chili lends heat, the lemon fresh acidity, and the toasted almonds a nice, thin textural crunch.

1 pound (450 g) broccoli
2 generous handfuls of arugula
Leaves from a bunch of fresh mint, shredded
1/2 cup (125 mL) olive oil
1 large onion, chopped
1 small garlic clove, crushed
1/2 teaspoon chili flakes
Zest of 1 lemon and a squirt of juice
Fleur de sel and freshly ground pepper
2 handfuls of toasted slivered almonds

Cut the broccoli stem(s) off very high up, right next to the florets, and set aside. Grate the head on the large holes of a box grater into a large bowl. Peel the stem(s) with a knife to remove the fibrous exterior, then, using a vegetable peeler, peel them into ribbons. Add to the grated broccoli along with the arugula and mint.

Heat the oil in a medium sauté pan and gently fry the onion until soft, about 8 minutes. Add the garlic and chili flakes for the last minute. Stir onions and oil into the broccoli. Add the lemon zest. Season with lemon juice, salt, and pepper. Tumble into a serving dish and scatter over the toasted almonds. Serve.

MAKES: 6 SERVINGS

EASY ARTICHOKES
with "BASTARD SAUCE"

I know you think artichokes are a pain, but in this particular instance their preparation is so unintimidating that I've even done them for a crowd. The usual pre-cook trimming is sidestepped, and the artichokes are simply boiled whole. Once they're done, just split them lengthwise and scoop out the chokes with a spoon. And what, you might ask, is *sauce bâtarde*? What you have is a cheater's version of classic hollandaise with some of the flavourings of sauce béarnaise. Leftover sauce can be refrigerated and gently warmed the next day in a warm-water bath for a few minutes until it returns to a sauce consistency. If you can't be bothered with sauce, simply serve the artichokes with melted butter for dipping.

2 large globe artichokes	1 teaspoon Dijon mustard
1/2 lemon	1/2 cup (110 g) butter, melted
1 egg yolk	Salt and pepper
1 tablespoon tarragon vinegar	A handful of fresh tarragon leaves, chopped

Pull off any small bottom leaves from the artichokes and trim the stems down to the white flesh. Rub the cut surfaces with the lemon. Take a pot large enough to hold the artichokes, fill it with salted water, and bring to a boil. Squeeze the lemon juice into it and drop in the squeezed lemon. Add the artichokes and simmer until tender when tested with a knife, about 45 minutes.

Drain the artichokes. Cut them in half lengthwise with a bread knife, then use a spoon to scrape out the feathery chokes. Arrange the artichokes cut side up on a platter and turn your attention to the sauce.

In a small bowl, whisk together the yolk, vinegar, and mustard, then season with salt and pepper. Whisk in the melted butter in a thin stream. Taste and adjust the seasonings, adding lemon juice to taste. Stir in the tarragon.

Pass the sauce with the platter of artichokes. The sauce can be spooned into the well where the choke was. Pull off the leaves and dip them into the sauce with your fingers. The heart and stem are eaten with knife and fork.

MAKES: 4 SERVINGS

MUSHROOMS *en* PAPILLOTE

A friend from serious mushroom territory taught me this trick, and I now think it's one of the best ways to cook mushrooms. I had gone over for dinner just as *trompettes de la mort* ("trumpets of death," so named because they are shaped like trumpets and black) hit the markets. When something is perfectly in season and you're eating it for the first time in ages, it's worth turning to a recipe that enhances the flavour to the maximum, which this one does. Hermetically sealed as they are, the mushrooms' flavour has nowhere to escape. Serve with slices of toasted baguette rubbed with garlic and butter.

1-1/4 pounds (565 g) assorted wild mushrooms
A drizzle of olive oil
Salt and finely ground pepper
3 garlic cloves, thinly sliced
2 tablespoons butter
A handful of chopped fresh parsley

Heat the oven to 375°F (190°C). Cut 4 rectangles of parchment (about one and a half times as large as a piece of standard letter-sized paper) and lay them on the counter.

Toss the mushrooms with a drizzle of olive oil, then season with salt and pepper. Divide them among the parchment pieces, placing them on the bottom half of each sheet. Scatter over the garlic, put pinches of butter on top of each, and scatter over the parsley. Fold the parchment over to cover the mushrooms, then, starting at the folded end, fold and twist the open edges to seal each package completely. At the end, twist to secure. The packages must be *completely* sealed. Lay them on a baking sheet. Bake for 10 minutes.

Transfer the packages to plates and serve immediately, having your guests cut open their own packages.

MAKES: 4 SERVINGS

WHITE ASPARAGUS
with ALMOND CREAM

A very elegant, monochromatic first course. White asparagus is a great delicacy, and this mild, pale, earthy-textured sauce is a perfect match because it doesn't overwhelm. Assume three asparagus spears per person if they're on the thinner side and two per person if you're lucky enough to get your hands on the nice big fat ones.

1 tablespoon butter

1 garlic clove, chopped

1 small onion, chopped

1 cup (250 mL) heavy cream

3 tablespoons white wine

2 ounces (55 g) slivered blanched almonds

Salt and pepper

A few squeezes of lemon juice

16 to 24 fat white asparagus spears, trimmed and peeled

A handful of sliced almonds, lightly toasted

For the sauce, put the butter, garlic, onion, cream, wine, and almonds in a saucepan. Boil until reduced by one-third, 8 to 10 minutes. Cool slightly, then purée in a blender. Season with salt, pepper, and lemon juice. The sauce should be thick, but if it's too thick, thin it with a bit of cream.

Bring a large sauté pan of water to a boil. Salt it and add a squeeze of lemon juice. Add the asparagus and simmer until tender, 10 to 20 minutes, depending on the thickness. Drain and rinse in cold water to stop the cooking. Pat dry with a clean tea towel.

Arrange the asparagus on a platter and spoon over the sauce. Scatter over the sliced almonds and serve.

MAKES: 8 SERVINGS

Kitchen Towels

I have a terrible habit of making completely inappropriate purchases on my travels. It's fair to say that if you're passing through Vancouver en route to Paris via Korea, then the notion of trotting into a Salvation Army shop and emerging with a 20-year-old food processor is not a particular sign of smarts. However, sometimes you have to grab things when you see them. For example, I don't regret that once, in Chicago on a restaurant-hopping weekend, I was suddenly struck with a panicked need to equip myself with a lifetime supply of flour-sack tea towels. *That* was not fool-hardy, say what you like, because they are the best tea towels I've ever known! Soft, absorbent, big...

I'd like to imagine that, one day, I'm going to get it together enough to have a serious tea towel system going in the kitchen. On one hook, a hand towel, and it would have to look unmistakably like one, something marginally fluffy, perhaps even with a design of handprints all over it to remove all doubt about its purpose. It wouldn't end there. A simple flour-sack towel suits me for drying dishes, but it's a towel for drying glasses where I'm still waiting for my prince. It would be lovely to find a large, absorbent, lint-free towel that dries and polishes glasses until they gleam. Some wineglass companies sell such things, but they're always ugly and stamped with a hideous logo. So I'm still on the lookout...

LINGUINE *with* CHERRY TOMATO SAUCE

The key to this recipe is toasting the garlic to a nutty golden brown, as it gives the overall dish a rather charming moodiness. I love the barely-there but warming creamy feel of this unusual tomato sauce.

1/4 cup (60 mL) olive oil
2 to 3 garlic cloves, chopped
Pinch chili flakes
1-1/2 pounds (675 g) cherry tomatoes
Salt and pepper
1/4 cup (60 mL) white wine
1/2 cup (125 mL) chicken stock
14 ounces (400 g) linguine
A few handfuls of shredded fresh basil

Heat the oil in a large sauté pan. Add the garlic and cook, stirring occasionally, until golden, 2 to 3 minutes. Add the chili flakes and the tomatoes. Season with salt and pepper. Cover and sweat over low heat until the tomato skins are very loose, about 15 minutes. Pluck the skins off with tongs and discard. Press the tomatoes with the back of a spoon to crush just slightly. Add the wine and stock. Simmer until reduced to sauce consistency, about 20 minutes.

Bring a large pot of water to a boil. Salt it and add the pasta. Cook until al dente. Drain the pasta and toss it with the sauce and the basil. Serve immediately.

MAKES: 6 TO 8 FIRST-COURSE SERVINGS OR 4 MAIN-COURSE SERVINGS

BOW TIES *with*
MUSHROOMS *and* BASIL

This is a surprisingly scrumptious pasta dish that a Paris neighbour once served to me as a last-minute supper. (Yes, it's true, even the French resort to pasta sometimes.) In place of crème fraîche, you can use equal parts sour cream and heavy cream, which is different but also good. If bow ties put you off for any reason (But why? They're so much fun!), use orecchiette instead.

1 pound (450 g) bow tie pasta
2 tablespoons olive oil
1 pound (450 g) shiitake or button mushrooms, trimmed and thinly sliced
1/2 cup (125 mL) crème fraîche
Salt and pepper
2 to 3 handfuls of fresh basil leaves, shredded

Bring a large pot of water to a boil, salt it, and cook the pasta until al dente.

Meanwhile, heat the oil in a sauté pan over medium-high heat and fry the mushrooms until tender, 5 to 7 minutes. Stir in the crème fraîche, heat through, and season with salt and pepper.

Drain the pasta and toss it with the creamy mushrooms and the basil. Serve immediately.

MAKES: 8 FIRST-COURSE SERVINGS

SWISS CHARD "RISOTTO"

A chic and novel way to serve chard, wherein the stems become "rice," bathed in a fragrant, leaf-flecked broth with a crisp bacony wheel on top.

1 bunch of Swiss chard (about 1 pound/450 g)
A squeeze of lemon juice
2 tablespoons butter
1 tablespoon olive oil
1 onion, minced
1/4 cup (60 mL) white wine
1-1/2 cups (375 mL) rich chicken stock
1 cup (40 g) finely grated Parmesan cheese
Salt and pepper
4 thin slices capocollo, prosciutto, or crisp-fried pancetta

Trim the ends of the chard stems, then separate the leaves from the stems. Roll up the leaves, thinly slice, and set aside. Chop the stems into pieces the size of rice. Toss with a squeeze of lemon juice and set aside.

Heat the butter and oil in a large sauté pan and gently fry the onion until translucent, about 5 minutes. Stir in the chopped stems, pour in the wine and chicken stock, and simmer until tender, about 5 minutes. Stir in the sliced leaves, cover, and simmer until tender, about 2 minutes. Uncover and reduce the liquid a little if necessary: it should not be soupy, but you do want some liquid. Stir in the cheese and season with salt and pepper.

Ladle into soup plates and set alongside a rosette of capocollo or prosciutto, or a slice of fried pancetta.

MAKES: 4 SERVINGS

Salt and Pepper

Salt and pepper shakers are a silly invention, if you ask me. It's impossible to tell how much salt is coming out of a shaker and I can't bear that lack of control. As for pepper shakers, any pepper powdery enough to fit through those fine holes is not worth shaking out in the first place.

In the kitchen, I have separate pots for salts: one for fine, one for coarse, one for Maldon or fleur de sel. For the table, I like to change the salt vessel, depending on how the table is set, but it's always some sort of pot (sometimes as simple as half an oyster shell). Pepper is in a small grinder of high quality. (If I've learned anything in this life, it's that a cheap pepper grinder will get you nowhere, except on to the next cheap pepper grinder which will be swiftly followed by the next...)

Since it's maddening to have salt and pepper separated at the table, it's not a bad idea to have a little tray to put both on. That way, when people ask for the salt, you can pass the little tray instead and keep the bride and groom together.

BUCKWHEAT NOODLES *with* CAVIAR

One Paris friend swears by spaghetti tossed in butter and mentaiko (Japanese-style marinated cod roe), an ingredient easy to find in the Japanese grocers in the 1st arrondissement. Another friend, from Provence, boasts a favourite dish of pasta tossed with shaved poutarge (cured fish roe, also called bottarga), lemon zest, parsley, olive oil, and plenty of pepper. I like both as celebratory first courses, but perhaps top on my list is this one, which, because of the high price of caviar, I reserve for special evenings such as New Year's Eve. When you think of it, it's really a variation on caviar and blini, only without the trouble of frying up blini.

Salt
4 ounces (110 g) wheat-and-buckwheat or 100% buckwheat soba noodles
2 tablespoons butter, melted
2 handfuls of chopped fresh chives
1 tin (1 ounce/30 g) caviar (more, if you're feeling seriously flush)
Sour cream or crème fraîche, for serving (optional)

Bring a large pot of water to a boil. Salt it, add the pasta, and lightly boil until al dente, 6 to 7 minutes. Drain.

Immediately toss with the butter and chives and twirl onto serving plates. Top each mound with a spoonful of caviar and serve immediately, passing the sour cream for those who like it (although, personally, I like how clean the dish tastes without it).

MAKES: 4 FIRST-COURSE SERVINGS

GRILLED PRAWNS *and* RADICCHIO *with* BAGNA CAUDA

A lively way to begin a feast, what with the bitterness from the grilled radicchio rubbing shoulders with a buttery sauce that's spiked with garlic, anchovy, and capers. Grilled scallops can replace prawns, if you prefer. Either way, it's a relatively substantial first course, so go light on the second, or simply make this the main.

For the sauce
1/2 cup (125 mL) olive oil
6 garlic cloves, grated
8 anchovies, rinsed, minced, and mashed
1 tablespoon capers, chopped
1/4 cup (55 g) butter, cut into cubes
A handful of chopped fresh parsley

For the prawns and radicchio
1 head radicchio (about 9 ounces/250 g),
    cut into 8 wedges
9 ounces (250 g) prawns, peeled and deveined
1 tablespoon grapeseed oil
Salt and pepper
Lemon wedges, for garnish

Make the sauce by mixing together in a saucepan the oil, garlic, anchovies, and capers. Set over very low heat for 10 minutes so the flavours commingle and mellow. Remove from the heat and whisk in the butter a piece at a time so that it blends into the sauce, whisking until each piece of butter is absorbed before adding the next. Stir in the parsley. Keep warm in a sauceboat.

Heat a large dry cast-iron skillet or grill over medium-high heat. Briskly fry the radicchio on both cut sides until darkened and slightly wilted, about 30 seconds per side. Remove to a serving platter.

Toss the prawns in the grapeseed oil. Season with salt and pepper. Fry in the same pan until pink and just cooked through, about 1 minute per side. Remove to the platter of radicchio and drop around the lemon wedges. Pass the sauce separately.

MAKES: 4 SERVINGS

GLAM CLAMS

This is an ultra-easy yet impressive and convivial dish for a crowded table. If you'd like a truly different embellishment, I alert you to the bread beignets recipe on p. 270. A friend makes a savoury version without sugar and smears them with Korean chili paste before tossing them on the clams—a great way to mop up the scrumptious juices. A word about razor clams: be sure to buy them from a reliable fishmonger who will have cleaned them properly, otherwise they'll be full of sand. If they need any additional treatment, the fishmonger should be able to tell you.

2 tablespoons butter
4 garlic cloves, minced
1 pound (450 g) razor clams, scrubbed
1 pound (450 g) small clams, scrubbed
1/2 cup (125 mL) white wine
Salt and pepper
Zest of 1 lemon
A couple of handfuls of chopped fresh parsley

Melt the butter in a large skillet or pot over medium-high heat. Add the garlic and cook, stirring, for 1 minute. Dump in the clams, pour over the wine, and season with salt and pepper. Cover, reduce heat to medium, and steam until clams open, about 5 minutes. Discard any clams that haven't opened.

Tumble the lot onto a serving platter. Strew over the lemon zest and parsley. Serve.

MAKES: 8 SERVINGS

EASY OYSTERS

I love oysters almost any way, but as a hostess it's certainly with their cooked form that I'm most at ease. Even the normally oyster-squeamish seem to like them that way, and certainly those who are allergic to the job of shucking (ahem . . . *moi*) are happy because with this clever method the oven pops them open effortlessly. Buy oysters from a reputable source, making sure that each oyster is tightly shut (or at least shuts quickly when tapped), and keep refrigerated (flat side up in a bowl, covered with a damp tea towel) until ready to bake. These are delicious as an appetizer. I've also brought out a platter to serve as an amusing accompaniment to soup.

12 medium oysters

3 tablespoons butter, melted

1 garlic clove, crushed

1 tablespoon Pernod or white wine (optional)

A handful of very finely chopped fresh parsley

About 1/4 cup (15 g) large dry bread crumbs or panko

Heat the oven to 425°F (220°C). Set the oysters flat side up on a baking sheet. Bake until the shells lift open like parting lips, about 5 minutes. Remove them as they open. (They may not all open at the same time and they won't necessarily gape, so keep a close eye—you don't want to actually cook them.) When they're all out, raise the oven rack and heat the broiler.

Slide a sharp knife into the opening of each oyster and glide it along the top (flat) shell to release the oyster from its muscle. Discard the top shell and pour off any oyster liquor. Set the oysters, on their half shells, back on the baking sheet.

Toss together the butter, garlic, Pernod, parsley, and bread crumbs. Sprinkle over the oysters. Broil until the crumbs start to brown, a matter of minutes. Serve hot.

MAKES: 4 SERVINGS

Scullery Fantasies

I know I am entirely alone in this, but indulge me, will you? I *like* doing dishes (and I have a dream of how I'd like doing dishes even more). I love the comforting, homey feel of warm, soapy water up to my elbows. I love my head getting lost in daydreams while my hands are on automatic. I especially relish the satisfaction of watching order emerge, as if by magic, from wine-, crumb-, and sauce-splattered chaos, right before my eyes! Concrete progress is what it is, and it's not every job that gives a person that. (Government officials should perhaps do dishes more often. It might save them their shrink bills!)

On to the fantasy: I really, really, really want a scullery. I don't mean I want to join the cast of *Downton Abbey* and become a sour-faced maid in some cold, dingy room off the cellar kitchen of a grand house. No, I want one in MY house, right off the kitchen. Imagine, a poetically quiet little room, possibly pale blue like a summer sky, completely devoted to washing and storing dishes. It could very well turn out to be my favourite room in the house! I love dishes and glasses and cut-lery, after all. I could pore over cupboards of them all day, imagining what to put in and on them for future feasts.

A scullery (and I have, in fact, been in quite a number of lovely old houses that have them) is, contrary to expectations, generally a very peaceful place. Often there's a window that looks out over a lawn or towards a quiet plot of trees, and there you can stand, swivelling a chamois around water glasses whilst you stare into space until someone comes along and smacks you to alert you to the fact that the phone is ringing. (I mean, in today's world, I'd say being able to achieve this kind of state without a yogi at hand or some sort of expensive drug must be pure luxury!)

The idea of a scullery in Paris is idiotic. Every kitchen I've ever had there has been the size of a broom closet—even in grand apartments, kitchens are, surprisingly, the last thought—so the notion of having a whole separate space with a double porcelain sink skirted with a flowery curtain of fabric beneath it and walls of plate racks for arranging patterned platters one by one, wooden slats for sliding wine-glasses into upside down in rows is . . . well, I did say this was a fantasy!

MUSSELS *in* SAFFRON CREAM

We all love classic *moules marinières*, but there are occasions when we prefer not to get our hands messy. This elegant recipe is a pinch to make, and it can be prepared ahead of time for last-minute reheating. Serve with baguette and follow with a light main course.

2 pounds (900 g) mussels
1/2 cup (125 mL) white wine
2 teaspoons butter
1 shallot, minced
1 garlic clove, crushed
A generous pinch of saffron, lightly crushed
2 teaspoons flour
1/4 cup (60 mL) heavy cream
A handful of chopped fresh chives

Discard any mussels that are open. Scrub and debeard the remaining mussels. Put them in a large pot with the wine and set them over medium-high heat. Bring to a boil, cover, and steam until they open, 3 to 4 minutes. Strain, reserving the cooking juices (you should have about a cup/250 mL). Set juices aside. Discard any mussels that haven't opened.

Remove the mussels from the shells, placing the meat in a bowl and discarding the shells.

Melt the butter in a small saucepan. Add the shallot, garlic, and saffron and gently sauté until shallot is soft, about 5 minutes. Sprinkle over the flour and cook, stirring, for 1 minute. Pour over the reserved cooking juices, stir to blend, then boil to reduce for 5 minutes. Add the cream; gently boil until reduced to soup consistency, 3 to 5 minutes. Add the mussels.

Gently warm through the mussels. Spoon the mussels into serving dishes, then pour over the sauce. Scatter over the chives, and serve, passing the peppermill, but holding back on salt as the mussels will have provided enough already.

MAKES: 4 SERVINGS

SASHIMI MIO

Oh, how the Japanese love Paris, and how Parisians love things Japanese, not least of all the chefs and cooks, who can't seem to get enough of one another's tastes and techniques! It's not in this lifetime that I'll be mastering Japanese knife skills, but if I get my hands on very fresh fish, one of my favourite things to do is to cut it into thin slivery pieces, dress it lightly in the manner of a flat French salad, and eat it raw. For any raw fish and seafood, always seek out a trustworthy fishmonger who can advise you on quality and freshness. There are plenty of options to choose from that work brilliantly here: tuna, halibut, bass, scallops—even mackerel or sturgeon.

3 ounces (85 g) sushi-grade fish
3 or 4 tiny red radishes
2 or 3 green onions or a small bunch of fresh chives
A small handful of fresh coriander leaves, torn
1 lime or lemon
1/4 cup (60 mL) soy sauce
1/4 to 1/2 teaspoon wasabi paste (optional)

Keep the fish refrigerated until just before serving.

Using a very sharp knife, slice the fish into paper-thin slices and arrange in a single layer on a platter. Using the same knife or a mandoline, shave the radishes into see-through-thin slices and scatter over the fish. Thinly slice the green onions (or chop the chives) and scatter over the fish along with the coriander. Finally, grate the lime or lemon zest over everything.

Mix together the soy sauce and wasabi to taste in a small bowl. Serve alongside the fish.

MAKES: 2 SERVINGS

SOUSED HERRING SANDWICHES

One Christmas in Paris, it seemed as though every drinks party I attended was serving substantial open-faced Nordic sandwiches. Scandinavian food is in, apparently, and every fishmonger in Paris sells pickled herring, so these canapés are a breeze to make. Good party food, winter or summer.

1 pound (450 g) soused (matjes) herring

1 medium red onion, minced

1 crisp red apple, finely chopped

3/4 cup (175 mL) crème fraîche

2 tsp Dijon mustard

2 tsp sugar

Salt and pepper

Squares or rounds of rye bread

Coarsely chopped fresh dill, for garnish

Drain the herring, discarding any condiments, and coarsely chop. Toss with the onion, apple, crème fraîche, mustard, and sugar. Season with salt and pepper. Spoon onto rye bread and garnish with dill.

MAKES: ABOUT 12 CANAPÉS

MINTY SARDINE TARTINES

You can make these using grilled fresh sardines when they're available, but good-quality tinned sardines are just as lip-smackingly good. I can never eat enough of these, and neither can anyone else I've served them to.

6 large tinned sardines (about 2 tins), drained
12 thin slices of toasted baguette
Heaps of shredded fresh mint leaves
Olive oil
1 lemon
Fleur de sel and freshly cracked pepper

Cut each sardine in half lengthwise and remove the spine. Lay a fillet on each slice of baguette toast and pile the mint on top. Drizzle over olive oil. Grate over lemon zest to taste, then squeeze over a little lemon juice. Season with fleur de sel and freshly cracked pepper. Serve.

MAKES: 12 TARTINES TO SERVE 4 AS A FIRST COURSE

CHICKEN LIVER PÂTÉ
THAT I ACTUALLY WANT *to* EAT

This is a French recipe, obviously, but one that I took to France rather than brought back from there. Why? Because I *loathe* chicken livers. But the chicken liver pâté made by Chef Graham Pratt at a Toronto restaurant called The Gabardine is a concoction so blissfully good it makes even me weak in the knees. This makes a large terrine for a party, so feel free to halve the recipe if you want a little less.

1 pound (450 g) chicken livers

About 3/4 cup (175 mL) milk

1 cup (250 mL) white wine

1/2 cup (125 mL) brandy

2 shallots, minced

4 large fresh sage leaves, finely chopped

2 teaspoons finely chopped fresh thyme

1/8 whole nutmeg, grated

4 eggs, at room temperature

3/4 teaspoon salt

1 pound (450 g) unsalted butter, very soft

Place the chicken livers in a bowl and pour over enough of the milk to cover them. Cover and put them in the fridge for a night.

The next day, heat the oven to 325°F (160°C). Drain and rinse the livers; set aside. In a small saucepan, boil the wine, brandy, shallots, sage, thyme, and nutmeg until reduced to about 1/4 cup (60 mL), about 10 minutes. Pour the reduction into a blender and whiz until smooth. Add the livers and whiz again. Add the eggs and salt, then whiz until the mixture is perfectly smooth. Now whiz in the butter, a piece at a time, until the mixture is perfectly smooth and amalgamated. If it looks curdled, you have not blended long enough, so keep going. Scrape into a 4-cup (1 L) terrine and bake in a water bath until just set, about 40 minutes.

Remove terrine from the water bath and cool completely. Cover and refrigerate for several hours. Serve with thinly sliced toasted baguette.

MAKES: ONE 4-CUP (1 L) TERRINE

LARD PASTRY

Parisians rarely use lard, which is a shame, because this recipe makes a layered crisp and flaky pastry that is right out of this world. (Mutual friends of the recipe's originator are so enamoured of it that they have it writ large and taped to their kitchen wall in Paris!) So what is an English pastry recipe doing in a French book? It's a poke in the ribs. The French can't stand the idea of the English being better at them in anything in the food department, and this recipe gives them a run for their money. If you find yourself in Paris looking for lard, ask your butcher for *saindoux.*

3 cups (375 g) flour
2 tablespoons sugar (only for sweet shells)
Pinch salt
1 cup (225 g) frozen lard, coarsely chopped
3/4 cup (175 mL) ice-cold water

Put everything except the water in a food processor and pulse a few times to make fine crumbs. Pour in the water and whiz until the dough comes together, about 10 seconds. It will be quite wet, which is just fine. Immediately spill onto plastic wrap. Pat into a rough ball, cut into 2 equal parts, pat each into a disc, wrap in plastic wrap, and refrigerate for at least an hour to rest.

Flour a surface, heavily or lightly depending on the wetness of the dough, and roll out the dough to use however you like.

Lard has a higher heating point than butter and can be baked, fearlessly, at higher temperatures. If you're making a double-crust pie, brush the top crust with egg glaze (an egg beaten with a teaspoon of water) and then scatter over a handful of sugar (for sweet pies) or a sprinkling of fleur de sel (for savoury ones). Bake lard tarts and pies at 400°F (200°C) until they're a deep golden brown, about 40 minutes.

MAKES: 2 LARGE ROUNDS OF PASTRY

MUSHROOM TART *with* TARRAGON *and* SMOKED GOUDA

This delicious and unusual tart is quite rich, so what I like is to make a big rectangle and cut it into squares to have with drinks. For a light supper, set it out with soup.

1/2 recipe for lard pastry (p. 71)
1 pound (450 g) button mushrooms, sliced
1 tablespoon butter
1 tablespoon olive oil
2 pink shallots, minced
1 garlic clove
3 ounces (85 g) smoked Gouda, thinly sliced
Salt and pepper
A handful of fresh tarragon leaves, coarsely chopped

Heat the oven to 400°F (200°C). On a lightly floured surface, roll out the pastry into a large rectangle. Lay it flat on a baking sheet.

Place the mushrooms in a large bowl. In a small skillet, heat the butter and oil and gently fry the shallots for about 3 minutes. Add the garlic and fry, stirring, for 1 minute. Pour the shallots over the mushrooms and toss with your hands to coat.

Lay the cheese slices over the pastry. Top with the mushrooms, distributing them evenly and right out to the edge of the pastry. Season with salt and pepper. Bake until the pastry is crisp, about 30 minutes. Scatter over the tarragon, cut into squares, and serve.

MAKES: 1 TART

Kitchen Conversation

Life would certainly be a lot less interesting if refrigerator magnets had never been invented. Think of how much you can learn about people with just one quick scan of the door of their Frigidaire! You know when they're driving children to soccer games, who needs to have a tooth pulled and on what day and by whom, that they've run out of toilet paper and icing sugar, that somebody called Arthur has sent them a postcard from Greece . . . It's not like a painting on the wall, ever fixed. Oh no, the fridge door changes constantly, a veritable living biography. One minute it boasts a kindergarten painting of the family in a single primary colour with everyone's legs coming straight out of their heads, the next minute there's a speeding ticket stuck up there, both by the same person. What greater missed opportunity could there ever be than a fridge door with nothing on it?

Now, a chalkboard, since we're inadvertently on the topic of kitchen communication systems, is a great thing to have on the go as well. I was at my most efficient in one Paris kitchen thanks to its enormous blackboard. I never forgot I'd run out of anything because I'd have that vast and convenient spot to write a list. And it was as good as texting when it came to letting people know where I was. "Off for apéro with C! Soup on stove! x, L." It's hard to find a decent blackboard these days, but I know there's some sort of paint available that works a treat. You can paint the whole kitchen door with it, if you want, or a big patch of wall, and—presto!—pass the chalk. I know several Parisians with a blackboard bit of wall.

A mirror may not exactly be a mode of communication, but it is a kitchen surface that reflects life back to us in occasional flashes. When I was growing up, we had a narrow mirror in the kitchen, above the double porcelain sink between two windows. I'm not quite sure why it had been put there, nor do I remember when it was taken down—some rash move in a renovation, no doubt, which was a mistake. It's not that anyone ever stood in front of it adjusting a collar or inspecting teeth, but for some reason, there was something very reassuring about that small mirror in just that place. I suppose you'd catch the odd glimpse of yourself off guard, as you filled the tea kettle or reached out to swat a fly, and it was kind of nice to be reminded that you were there.

RED ONION TART

This is a scrumptious and very pretty flat tart to serve with drinks or to plunk onto the table to have with a first-course soup.

1 all-butter puff pastry sheet (10 inches/25 cm square), thawed if frozen
3 tablespoons crème fraîche
3 tablespoons fresh chèvre
1 to 2 tablespoons Dijon mustard
1 large red onion, sliced paper thin
Salt and pepper
A handful of fresh thyme leaves

Heat the oven to 375°F (190°C). Keeping your puff pastry on its parchment, roll it out a bit thinner to make a rough rectangle, and slide it on its parchment onto the baking sheet. Prick all over with a fork.

Stir together the crème fraîche, chèvre, and mustard to taste until smooth. Spread over the pastry, going right out to the edges. Scatter over the onion (don't overdo it—you may not need all of it). Season with salt and pepper.

Bake until the crust is crisp and golden, about 25 minutes. Sprinkle over the thyme leaves and serve.

MAKES: 1 TART

MAIN C

OURSES

MAIN COURSES

Fines Herbes Omelette 81

Tomato Eggs 82

Green Eggs and Ham 83

Poached Eggs on Potato Rösti 84

Leftover Cheeses Soufflé 85

Croque Monsieur with Bluffer's Béchamel 90

Zucchini Tourte 91

Tuna Tart 94

Tartiflette with Camembert 95

Fresh Cheese and Herb Tart with Bread Crumb Crust 97

Simply Salmon 100

Sea Bass with Spring Mushrooms and Fava Beans 102

Potato-Crusted Cod with Anchovy Sauce 103

Lemon Sole Goujons with Asianesque Rouille 107

Cod with Tomatoes, Olives, and Artichokes 108

Halibut Baked in Cream 109

Fish Sausages 112

Lobster with Red Lentils 113

Curried Blanquette of Scallops 116

Spring Chicken in a Pan 117

Expats' Christmas Dinner Salad 120

Chicken and Endives in Cider Sauce 121

Chicken and Orange Tagine 122

Rôtisserie Chicken Dinner 126

Seared Duck with Plum Compote 127

Rosemary-Marinated Quail 129

Cordon Bleu Croquettes 130

Pantry Duck Parmentier 133

Bavette with Herb Butter 135

Steak Tartare 137

Beautiful Côte de Boeuf 139

Viennese Veal Cutlet 140

Fork and Spoon Lamb with Minty Yogurt Sauce 141

Veal Fricassée with Mushrooms 144

The Speediest of Lamb Chops 147

Choucroute Garnie à la Me 148

Pork Roast with Mustard Sauce 149

Gypsy Pork Boulettes 153

FINES HERBES OMELETTE

A French omelette is a very elegant thing, nothing to do with the trucker-sized omelettes from the other side of the Atlantic with their button-popping fillings. (Not that there isn't a place for those . . . there just isn't a place *here*.) No, a French omelette is a lady of a dish, as slender as a glove, perfect with a glass of wine and a little salad when you're dining alone or *à deux*.

4 or 5 gorgeous fresh eggs from a market

Salt and pepper

A knob of butter, plus extra for rubbing

A handful of chopped fresh fine herbs, such as chervil, tarragon, parsley, or chives

A small handful of grated Gruyère, if you like

Crack the eggs into a bowl, season with salt and pepper, and stir them with a fork. Set a nonstick pan over medium heat and melt the butter. When it's sizzling gently, add the eggs and cook, stirring with the fork for the first minute or so, until they start to set.

Now scatter over the herbs and cheese. Cover and cook for a minute or two to set the eggs. The French consider an omelette done when it is still slightly runny on top.

When the omelette is cooked to your liking, roll the omelette like a carpet using the fork, and tip it onto the plate. Rub the surface with butter, to make it glisten, and serve.

MAKES: 2 SERVINGS

TOMATO EGGS

Here's a cheerful impromptu supper for two. The piment d'Espelette gives just the right amount of heat to make the sauce exciting. Have a baguette on hand for mopping it up.

1 tablespoon olive oil
1 tablespoon butter
2 garlic cloves, crushed or thinly sliced
1-3/4 cups (425 mL) crushed tomatoes or tomato purée
Salt and black pepper
A few pinches of piment d'Espelette
4 eggs
A handful of chopped fresh parsley

Heat the oil and butter in a sauté pan until sizzling. Add the garlic and sauté, without browning, for about a minute. Add the tomatoes and season with salt, black pepper, and piment d'Espelette. Simmer, stirring occasionally, for 10 minutes. Crack the eggs on top of the tomatoes, then season. Cover and poach until the eggs are set to your liking, about 4 minutes.

Scatter over the parsley and serve straight from the pan.

MAKES: 2 SERVINGS

GREEN EGGS *and* HAM

The tomato eggs on p. 82 are so trendy, I thought it might be nice to suggest a variation on the theme. Here's a creamy version with spinach and ham for storybook lovers.

1 pound (450 g) baby spinach or assorted cooking greens
1 tablespoon butter
1 small onion, minced
1 garlic clove, crushed
1 cup (250 mL) heavy cream
Salt and pepper
Pinch nutmeg
4 thin slices ham
4 eggs
Parmesan cheese, for grating

Put the spinach in a large sauté pan with 1/4 cup (60 mL) water, cover, and wilt over medium heat, a matter of minutes. Drain, squeeze dry, and chop. Set aside.

Melt the butter in the same pan and gently sauté the onion until translucent. Add the garlic and cook, stirring, for 1 minute. Stir in the spinach, pour over the cream, and season with salt, pepper, and nutmeg. Simmer until the cream is reduced to a thick sauce.

Using the back of a spoon, make 4 nests in the spinach mixture. Line each with a slice of ham, then crack an egg into each nest. Cover and simmer until the eggs are cooked through to your liking, about 5 minutes. Scatter over grated Parmesan cheese, grind over black pepper, and serve.

MAKES: 4 SERVINGS

POACHED EGGS *on* POTATO RÖSTI

A poached egg is a treat, something to enjoy when you need a little TLC. The soft texture is perfect against a crunchy rösti, and the pairing makes a complete meal, which you can always round out with a bit of creamed chard or spinach or a slice of fried tomato.

For the rösti
1 medium Yukon Gold potato (about 5 ounces/140 g)
Salt and black pepper
Pinch cayenne pepper
1 tablespoon clarified butter, melted
2 tablespoons finely chopped fresh parsley

For the poached eggs
2 teaspoons tarragon vinegar
2 very fresh eggs

For the rösti, peel the potato and grate it on the large holes of a box grater. Salt it, then squeeze it in a tea towel to wring out the water. Empty the gratings into a bowl. Season with the black pepper and cayenne, then pour over the butter and add the parsley. Mix well, taste, and add more salt, if needed. Pat into 2 pancake shapes, about finger thick.

In a sauté or frying pan, bring 2 to 3 inches (5 to 8 cm) water to a boil for the poached eggs.

Meanwhile, heat another frying pan over medium-high heat. When the pan is hot, fry the rösti, turning once, until golden and very crisp on the outside and tender within, about 3 minutes per side. Season with salt and pepper. Keep warm.

When the egg water has come to a boil, stir in the vinegar. Turn off the heat and crack the eggs in, holding them close to the surface of the water as you do so. Do not touch them or move them around—just put on a lid and wait 2 to 3 minutes, by which time the whites should be opaque and the yolks still runny. Remove the eggs with a slotted spoon to paper towels to drain. Trim off any messy bits at the edges with a knife.

Transfer the rösti to warm plates and top each with an egg. Season with salt and pepper. Serve.

MAKES: 2 SERVINGS

LEFTOVER CHEESES SOUFFLÉ

One of my greatest soapbox speeches is the one about how soufflés are a brilliant suppertime solution when the cupboards seem bare. It's true! Why doesn't anyone believe me? This particular recipe is a great ego booster, too, because it's ultra-creamy and volcanically high-rising and fluffy.

1-1/4 cups (300 mL) milk

1 bay leaf

1/2 small onion or a split garlic clove

2 tablespoons fine dry bread crumbs or
   finely grated Parmesan cheese

2 tablespoons butter

1/4 cup (30 g) flour

1/2 teaspoon Dijon mustard

3 eggs, separated

2 egg whites

5 ounces (140 g) leftover cheeses, grated

Salt and pepper

Pinch cayenne pepper

Heat the milk in a saucepan with the bay leaf and onion. Just before it all boils over, turn the heat off, cover, and set aside to infuse for about 10 minutes.

Meanwhile, put the rack a third of the way from the bottom of the oven and heat the oven to 400°F (200°C). Butter a 4-cup (1 L) soufflé dish or other baking dish. Dust the bottom and sides with the bread crumbs or Parmesan cheese, tipping out any excess.

Discard the bay leaf and onion from the milk. Melt the butter in a medium saucepan over medium heat. When it stops foaming, whisk in the flour and cook, whisking, for 1 minute. Do not let the mixture brown. Gradually whisk in the warm milk and cook, whisking, until thick, a matter of minutes. Remove from the heat and whisk in the mustard, then the egg yolks, 1 at a time. Stir in all but a handful of the cheese. Season well with salt, pepper, and cayenne.

In a large bowl, whisk the egg whites to soft peaks with a pinch of salt. Fold a spoonful of the whites into the cheese mixture, then pour the cheese mixture over the remaining whites and gently fold to amalgamate. Pour the mixture into the soufflé dish. Scatter over the remaining cheese. Bake until puffed and golden brown, about 25 minutes. Serve immediately.

MAKES: 4 SERVINGS

The Niceness of Proper Napkins

Forgive me if this sounds precious, but there's nothing worse than sitting down to a fine meal and finding a flimsy, scratchy paper napkin to the left of your plate. Cloth napkins are the only way to go, and there's nothing about them that has to suggest formality or fuss. I have a friend in Paris who uses polka-dot handkerchiefs for napkins, for Pete's sake. And a typical bistro trick is to use traditional tea towels. (No need to iron cloth napkins, incidentally, unless you want to.)

I got a bit of an education in napkins when I lived in the French countryside. It was a big house with lots of people coming and going and a great deal of entertaining. Household members and guests were always asked to select a napkin ring for the duration of their stay, and the napkins would get changed only when they needed to be. Not every day, but, say, every few. The practice becomes rather interesting, really, because you soon discover that everyone folds his napkin in a distinctive way and it becomes a bit of a personality test...

Anyway, what I was going to say is that the key to napkin rings is to make sure no two in the house are alike. Unless you're a real expert in how every single person folds their napkin, with identical napkin rings you never know whose is whose. Some distinctive, identifying mark on each is a godsend. At the house in the countryside, the napkin rings were Russian, each with an image from a fairy tale on the side, so you knew if you were the wolf, or the girl with the milk pail, or the starry sky. Colours, numbers, words, shapes—there are plenty of ways to create sets that look like a family but aren't all quite the same.

Well, what a relief to have that off my chest. (I hope some manufacturers heard me.)

Anyway, when it comes to the napkins themselves, I don't think there are really any hard rules. I like them quite big, personally, and it's important that the fabric be natural and feel good against the skin. Cotton and linen, or some combination thereof, are the norm for good reason. I have a few sets of napkins that I had made for me a few years ago, out of yards of *toile de Jouy* procured in the fabric district of Paris. They have lasted eons and are still going strong and look good, but as I write this I'm thinking I might start expanding my collection just to shake things up. Who knows, I may even venture into polka-dot-handkerchief territory.

CROQUE MONSIEUR
with BLUFFER'S BÉCHAMEL

Most of the time these days, when you order croque monsieur in a bistro, all you get is a boring tartine of ham and cheese. Zzz . . . I prefer the old-fashioned way, which involved creamy béchamel, but I understand that takes an extra few seconds of effort. For the real thing: melt 2 tablespoons butter, whisk in a tablespoon of flour and cook for 1 minute, then pour over 1 cup (250 mL) milk and whisk a minute until thick. Season with salt and pepper and use this in place of the crème fraîche below—the crème fraîche being a cheat, but one that does result in a slightly faster tangy, creamy, hot sandwich that is ideal for lunch.

8 slices white bread
Butter, for spreading
Grainy Dijon mustard, for spreading
4 thin slices ham
1 cup (250 mL) crème fraîche
6 ounces (170 g) Gruyère, grated
Salt and pepper
A grating of nutmeg
Paprika, for sprinkling

Shift the rack to the top third of the oven and heat the oven to 450°F (230°C).

Butter the bread on one side only. Working in batches, fry in a frying pan on just the buttered side until golden and crisp, about a minute. Remove from the pan.

Arrange 4 slices toasted side down in a shallow baking dish. Spread with mustard. Lay a ham slice on each. Spread a heaping tablespoon of crème fraîche on each ham slice, then sprinkle with two-thirds of the cheese. Season with salt, pepper, and nutmeg.

Set the tops on the sandwiches, toasted side up. Spread the remaining crème fraîche on top, sprinkle over the remaining cheese, and dust with paprika. Bake until hot and bubbling, about 5 minutes. Eat with knife and fork, with a green salad alongside.

MAKES: 4 SERVINGS

ZUCCHINI TOURTE

Bright with curry and fresh with the cheese, this tart has substantial texture, not remotely quichey, which is why it's called "tourte" instead. (I have a vague feeling I made this one up . . .) No French person I know would agree, but I find whole wheat pastry preferable here to white. The one I make is: 1 cup + 2 tablespoons (140 g) whole wheat flour, 1/4 teaspoon salt, and 1/2 cup (110 g) cold butter whizzed in the food processor, then pulsed with 2 to 3 tablespoons ice-cold water for a few seconds to bind. It's always best if you let the pastry rest, wrapped, for an hour in the fridge before rolling.

Whole wheat pastry for single-crust 10-inch (25 cm) tart (see headnote)

2 tablespoons olive oil

1 onion, chopped

2 garlic cloves, minced

1 pound (450 g) zucchini (2 medium-small), grated

3 eggs

1/2 cup (125 mL) crème fraîche

5 ounces (140 g) fresh chèvre or cream cheese, softened

1 ounce (30 g) Parmesan cheese, finely grated

1 tablespoon curry powder

Salt and pepper

A handful of chopped fresh parsley

1 zucchini blossom (optional)

Heat the oven to 375°F (190°C). Roll out the pastry on a lightly floured surface to 1/4-inch (5 mm) thickness and line the bottom and sides of a 10-inch (25 cm) springform pan. Set it on a baking sheet.

Heat the oil in a sauté pan and fry the onion until soft, about 5 minutes. Stir in the garlic and zucchini and cook until tender, about 5 minutes. Remove from the heat.

In a medium bowl, whisk together the eggs, crème fraîche, chèvre, Parmesan cheese, and curry. Season with salt and pepper. Stir in the zucchini mixture and parsley. Taste and adjust the seasonings.

Pour the filling into the tart shell. Open out the petals of the zucchini blossom (if using) and lay the flower in the centre of the tart. Bake until set, about 30 minutes. Cool completely. Serve at room temperature.

MAKES: 6 SERVINGS

A Roast Chicken a Week
Can Change Your Life

We all need a default dinner for nights when we're too hassled to think, and for me that's roast chicken. It's so effortless that even if the only thing you've ever cooked in your life is instant coffee, you can pull it off. Heat the oven to 400°F (200°C). Season the bird with salt and pepper and put it in a roasting pan. Rub it with olive oil, dot it with butter, and pop it into the oven breast side down. An average bird will take an hour and a quarter; a chicken cut into pieces will take 35 to 45 minutes. When pierced with a knife at the leg joint and the juices run clear (that is, no traces of blood), it's done.

If you're not eating the chicken immediately, you can remove all the meat from the bones and save it for other uses in the week. Cold chicken is perfect for salads or sandwiches, but you can also heat the meat again by frying it in sizzling butter, transforming it into a hearty soup, or stirring it into béchamel for stuffing into crêpes or making into croquettes (p. 130). Those suggestions are just the tip of the iceberg.

A totally separate reason to roast a chicken a week is so you can make stock, which will take care of an entirely separate meal in the week, for example a risotto or rich soup of lentils and vegetables. Don't think about it, just make it one of your principles: whenever you roast chicken, prepare your stockpot at the same time. Here is how:

In the pot, put a halved onion, a peeled carrot, possibly a stick of celery, and a wad of parsley, a bay leaf, and 6 peppercorns. When the roasted bird comes out of the oven, remove it to a carving board and deglaze the roasting pan with 1/2 cup (125 mL) white wine or water, scraping up all the good bits on the bottom of the pan with a wooden spoon as you do so. Pour the liquid into the stockpot. Once the meat is off the bones, add all bones to the pot (including any you've salvaged from other people's plates). Cover with water, bring to a boil, reduce the heat, and simmer gently for 1-1/2 hours. Turn off the pot and let the stock cool. Strain it, and store the liquid in a jar in the refrigerator for up to three days, remembering to bring it to the boil again before using.

TUNA TART

The name doesn't sound overly promising, which is perhaps why I wobbled on the threshold when my friend asked if I'd like to stay for dinner because they'd be having this. Am I ever glad I did or I'd never have discovered this weeknight supper so simple yet satisfying it's worthy of a bottle of wine. A salad afterwards is all you need.

Pastry for single-crust 10-inch (25 cm) tart (p. 91)
2 tablespoons olive oil
2 large onions, very thinly sliced
2 tins (6 ounces/170 g each) tuna, drained
3/4 cup (175 mL) tomato purée
2 eggs
1/4 cup (60 mL) crème fraîche
Salt and black pepper
Pinch hot paprika or piment d'Espelette

Heat the oven to 400°F (200°C). Line a 10-inch (25 cm) tart pan with removable bottom with the pastry; trim the edges. Line the pastry with parchment paper and fill with dried beans. Bake for 12 minutes. Remove the parchment and beans. Return the pastry to the oven for 5 to 10 minutes or until cooked on the bottom but not colouring.

While the pastry is baking, prepare the filling: Heat the oil in a large sauté pan and gently fry the onions until soft, about 10 minutes. Stir in the tuna and tomato purée; cook until thick, about 10 minutes. Meanwhile, whisk together the eggs and crème fraîche. When the tuna mixture is ready, remove from the heat and whisk in the egg mixture to combine thoroughly. Season well with salt and black pepper. Add paprika to taste. Pour into the tart shell.

Bake until the filling is hot and firmly set and the pastry is crisp, about 30 minutes. Cool completely. Serve at room temperature.

MAKES: 4 TO 6 SERVINGS

TARTIFLETTE *with* CAMEMBERT

Reblochon cheese from the Savoyard is the classic cheese for this wintertime recipe, but outside France it can be hard to find, so I'm suggesting Camembert as a renegade replacement. You could also use grated hard cheese, such as Comté or Gruyère—even white Cheddar if you want to be a real rebel. A paella pan or a cast-iron frying pan works best here because the secret to a truly great tartiflette is to get a crisp, golden crust forming beneath the melting, creamy, potatoey, bacony top in the manner of a good paella. A big green salad, a big bottle of wine, a cold winter's night, a nice guy in a woolly sweater . . . what else do you need to be happy?

1-1/2 pounds (675 g) waxy potatoes	1/2 cup (125 mL) crème fraîche
1 tablespoon butter	1 round of Camembert (6 ounces/170 g)
1 tablespoon olive oil	Salt and pepper
1 onion, chopped	2 garlic cloves, crushed
4 ounces (110 g) bacon, julienned	Pinch nutmeg
2 tablespoons white wine	

Put the potatoes in a pot of salted water, bring to a simmer, and cook until they are just shy of being tender, about 20 minutes, depending on size. Drain, peel, and slice medium-thick.

Heat the butter and oil in a heavy frying pan over medium heat and gently cook the onion until softened, about 10 minutes. Add the bacon and cook, stirring occasionally, until cooked but not crisp, about 5 minutes. Deglaze the pan with the wine, and boil until the liquid has disappeared, about a minute. Gently stir in the sliced potatoes and crème fraîche.

Slice the cheese in half through the waist, then cut each half into quarters. Lay the cheese, cut side down, on top of the potatoes, and leave on the heat until melted, about 5 minutes. Season with salt and pepper, and stir in the garlic and nutmeg. Leave the pan on the heat, without stirring, until a crust forms on the bottom of the potatoes, about 15 minutes. Serve.

MAKES: 4 TO 6 SERVINGS

FRESH CHEESE *and* HERB TART
with BREAD CRUMB CRUST

The beauty of this fresh-tasting tart is that you don't have to fuss with pastry: bread crumbs and butter alone provide a beautiful golden casing. (It's essential to use large flaky bread crumbs, not the dry powdery stuff.) I love the irresistibly tangy creaminess of the filling, distracted by nothing but a serious smattering of fresh herbs (try all mint sometime, if you've got a glut of that, because it's fabulous here). Serve with green salad and some curls of cured ham on the side for lunch.

3 tablespoons butter, softened
About 1/2 cup (30 g) large homemade bread crumbs (p. 207)
4 eggs
1 cup (250 mL) faisselle (French fresh cheese) or ricotta cheese
1/2 cup (125 mL) crème fraîche or heavy cream
A few generous handfuls of mixed chopped fresh rosemary, chives, chervil, and parsley
Salt and pepper
4 ounces (100 g) Gruyère or other hard white cheese such as old Cheddar, grated

Heat the oven to 375°F (190°C). Smear the butter over the bottom and sides of a 9-inch (23 cm) springform pan. Scatter over the bread crumbs, then swirl the pan so the crumbs coat the bottom and sides. Press lightly with your hands so that they stay in place. *Voilà*—your crust!

Beat together the eggs, faisselle, and crème fraîche, then stir through the herbs. Season with salt and pepper. Pour filling into the "pastry" and scatter over the grated cheese. Bake until filling is set in the centre (it will no longer jiggle), about 25 minutes.

Set on a rack to cool for about 10 minutes so the edges pull away from the pan. Remove the sides and slide the tart onto a serving plate. Serve warm.

MAKES: ONE 9-INCH (23 CM) TART, ABOUT 6 SERVINGS

Apéritif Bar

I'm always in a bit of a fix if I don't have someone on hand to deal with pre-dinner drinks because when you're busy cooking it's impossible to run around filling glasses at the same time. In Paris, where the apéritif is a sacred part of dinner, this can be especially nerve-racking. What's a two-handed person to do?

One Parisian couple I know have the ideal solution: an open bar. And this is not because they have a bar (they don't), it's because they have brains. They just arrange a spot somewhere out of the cook's way—a shelf in the living room, a corner of counter—and like putting up a temporary nativity scene, they lay out a snack or two, some glasses, a few bottles on ice… Then when you come in, you simply help yourself and let the chef keep at putting the finishing touches on dinner.

SIMPLY SALMON

This is one of the best ways I've found for cooking salmon, and one of the simplest, known to the French as *saumon à l'unilatéral*, which unfortunately sounds rather like something off a construction site. Names aside, the method does leave the fish incredibly moist and the flavours pure. Serve it with boiled new potatoes tossed in butter, carrots under parchment (p. 172), and a salad of Italian parsley leaves dressed in olive oil and seasoned. I know it's very pared down, but sometimes this is just the sort of meal a body wants.

1 tablespoon butter
1 tablespoon olive oil
4 salmon fillets (about 4 ounces/110 g each)
Fleur de sel and freshly ground pepper

Heat the oil and butter in a frying pan until very hot. Lay in the salmon (skin side down, if it has skin). Fry for 2 minutes, then cover and continue cooking, checking occasionally, until the fish is just cooked through to the top, about 5 minutes. Do not flip the fish.

Transfer the fish to warm plates. Sprinkle with fleur de sel and freshly ground pepper.

MAKES: 4 SERVINGS

SEA BASS *with* SPRING MUSHROOMS *and* FAVA BEANS

This gorgeous spring dish takes just minutes to prepare. The only slight fiddling is with the fava beans, but there are so few it's really no sweat. Once they're shelled, blanch the beans in boiling salted water for 30 seconds to 1 minute. Drain and immediately rinse in ice-cold water, then pop them out of their husks. (Please don't substitute frozen edamame, which are hard, heavy, and lacking in the delicate flavour that this luxurious fish deserves.)

4 sea bass or halibut fillets (4 to 5 ounces/110 to 140 g each)
A splash of white wine
Salt and pepper
2 tablespoons butter
6 fresh morel mushrooms, cleaned
3 porcini mushrooms, thickly sliced
1/2 cup (200 g) shelled fava beans (from about 1 pound/450 g pods)
1/4 cup (60 mL) chicken stock

Heat the oven to 375°F (190°C). Set the fish in a cast-iron frying pan. Pour a splash of white wine around them. Season the fish with salt and pepper and dot the tops with 1 tablespoon of the butter. Bake until just tender: be vigilant after 5 minutes.

Meanwhile, melt the other tablespoon of butter in a sauté pan over medium-high heat and fry the mushrooms until tender, about 3 minutes. Add the fava beans at the end just to warm through. Remove from the heat and keep warm.

Transfer the fish to warm plates. Deglaze the pan with the stock and boil for a minute or two to thicken. Pour the jus over the fish. Scatter the mushrooms and fava beans around. Serve.

MAKES: 4 SERVINGS

POTATO-CRUSTED COD
with ANCHOVY SAUCE

A magical little Franco-Swedish number, wherein plain fish fillets get a crisp potato topping and bathe in a seductive anchovy-dill sauce. The Parisian-based Swede who gave me this dish is adamant that only Swedish-style anchovies will do, but I use regular ones and love the results.

For the sauce
1 tablespoon butter
2 shallots, chopped
1 teaspoon white vinegar
1/4 cup (60 mL) white wine
3/4 cup (175 mL) heavy cream
6 anchovies, chopped
A handful of chopped fresh dill

For the fish
2 waxy potatoes, peeled
Salt and pepper
2 tablespoons butter, melted
4 skinless cod fillets (5 ounces/140 g each)
1 tablespoon olive oil
A few dill fronds, for garnish

For the sauce, melt the butter in a large saucepan (large to prevent any boiling over later) and gently fry the shallots until they're soft and getting a little colour. Deglaze with the vinegar, then add the wine and cream. Boil down to sauce consistency, stir in the anchovies and dill, and keep warm.

For the fish, grate the potatoes lengthwise on a box grater. Do not rinse or dry. Season with salt and pepper and toss with the butter. Season the fish. Divide the potatoes among the fish fillets, spreading them over the tops and pressing to cover completely.

Heat the oil in a large frying pan. When very hot, lay the fillets in potato side down. Cook until the potatoes are golden and cooked through, about 5 minutes. Flip and finish the fish on the other side, a matter of minutes.

Divide the sauce among warm plates and set the fish on top, potato side up. Garnish with dill fronds and serve.

MAKES: 4 SERVINGS

Affordable Hostess Gifts

The best hostess gift I ever received was a gravy boat. And not just any gravy boat: this one, found in a Paris flea market by a friend of mine for four euros, had a spout on each end, one marked "m" and the other marked "g," the latter with a sort of porcelain throat down its inside leading to the bottom of the vessel. Now what a mystery this was! I learned that the "m" stood for *maigre* (lean) and the "g" stood for *gras* (fat). Why, it was a gravy boat designed in heaven for Jack Sprat (who'd eat no fat) and his wife (who'd eat no lean): anyone at the table who wanted less fat in the gravy poured from the "m" spout, which brought up the lean gravy from the bottom; whoever wanted extra-fatty gravy poured from the "g" side and got gravy from the top. (I've since learned that the English term for this is "gravy separator.") Genius!

Paris has flea markets year round, and you can often negotiate excellent deals. Another friend once gave me a Peugeot pepper grinder, large and in the shape of an antique coffee mill. But I'd be delighted with anything! A floral plate, perhaps, a mug, an old tin ladle, an antique mezzaluna . . . It's just as delightful to receive something personal like that with a bit of history as it is to receive a pricy bouquet of flowers or box of chocolates. So if you're low on funds and invited to dinner, do not stress. Start a gift drawer that you fill only with items under five dollars, cleverly found in flea markets. You'll be the talk of the town.

LEMON SOLE GOUJONS
with ASIANESQUE ROUILLE

We've got a bit of an Asianesque variation on rouille here for sauce, but feel free to go traditional if you prefer, or use tartar sauce, or even a mixture of Greek yogurt, lime juice, and chopped fresh coriander. If you aren't a sauce person, try these wonderfully crisp little morsels with just some lime juice squeezed over and a smattering of coriander leaves strewn on top.

For the sauce	*For the fish*
1 cup (250 mL) mayonnaise	1 pound (450 g) skinless whiting or lemon sole
3 tablespoons sambal oelek	Flour, for dredging
2 tablespoons lime juice	Salt and pepper
1 teaspoon tomato paste	1 egg
1 garlic clove, crushed	Peanut oil, for frying
Salt and pepper	Torn fresh coriander leaves, for garnish
	Lime wedges, for garnish

For the sauce, stir together the mayonnaise, sambal oelek, lime juice, tomato paste, garlic, and salt and pepper. Taste and adjust the seasonings.

Pat the fish dry. Slice it into finger strips. Put flour in a shallow dish and season it well with salt and pepper. In a second shallow dish, beat the egg.

Heat a good inch (2.5 cm) of oil in a deep sauté pan. When the oil is sizzling, working in batches, dip the fish in the seasoned flour to coat all sides and shake off any excess. Dip in egg, letting the excess drip off, then dip in the flour again. Lower the fish into the oil and fry until crisp and golden, 2 to 3 minutes. Remove to paper towels to drain and season with salt. Transfer to a serving platter. Scatter over coriander leaves and drop around a few wedges of lime. Pass the sauce separately.

MAKES: 4 SERVINGS

COD *with* TOMATOES, OLIVES, *and* ARTICHOKES

Summery-simple and evocative of southern France, this punchy dish needs nothing on the side, although boiled peeled potatoes, perhaps cooked with a few threads of saffron in the cooking water, round out the meal nicely.

About 2 tablespoons olive oil

1 thick piece cod (1-1/2 pounds/675 g), preferably back of cod

Salt and pepper

1 jar or tin (14 ounces/398 mL) artichoke hearts (not marinated), drained

6 ounces (170 g) cherry tomatoes, halved or quartered

About 2 ounces (55 g) sliced pitted black olives

About 2 tablespoons capers

A few generous handfuls of torn fresh parsley leaves

1 garlic clove, crushed

1/4 cup (60 mL) white wine

Zest of 1 lemon (optional)

Heat the oven to 375°F (190°C). Drizzle a little of the olive oil over the bottom of a baking dish that will accommodate the fish generously, then lay in the fish and season it with salt and pepper.

Scatter the artichoke hearts, tomatoes, olives, capers, and parsley leaves around the fish. Whisk the garlic into the remaining olive oil and pour over the fish, then pour over the wine. Season with salt and pepper. Sprinkle over the lemon zest (if using).

Pop into the oven and bake until the fish flakes at the touch of a fork, 15 to 25 minutes, depending on the thickness. Serve.

MAKES: 4 SERVINGS

HALIBUT BAKED *in* CREAM

Fish-savvy friends told me about this method of cooking halibut, a fish notoriously tricky because of its tendency to dry out very quickly. Here, however, it bakes in a protective bath of soy-scented cream, which results in flesh approaching the texture of butter.

2 bay leaves
1 piece skinless halibut (1 pound/450 g)
1 to 2 cups (250 to 500 mL) heavy cream
1 tablespoon soy sauce

Heat the oven to 350°F (180°C). Lay the bay leaves in a baking dish just large enough to accommodate the halibut. Set the fish on top. Pour over enough cream to cover and splash in the soy sauce.

Bake until the fish is tender and flakes at the touch of a fork, about 15 minutes. Serve.

MAKES: 4 SERVINGS

Cutting Boards

My collection of cutting boards is becoming so vast that soon I'll be able to build a house out of them. I use them not just for chopping but also sometimes as rustic serving platters, which explains why I have so many sizes. The most used board is a large, sturdy, rectangular wooden one that gives me plenty of room to manoeuvre and ensures that whatever I'm chopping isn't falling off the edges. I'm not a fan of small boards for chopping even small amounts, but they can be nice to eat something like a sandwich from instead of a plate, for a change.

Let it be said that no plastic or glass cutting board will ever enter my hallowed halls. They're bad for knives, unattractive to look at, and not as hygienic as wood (that's a fact). I wash my wooden boards by hand with soap and water, then dry them right away with a towel and stand them up on end so they can dry out completely in the air. Occasionally, I rub them with oil, too, for a little beauty treatment. Some are old and some are young and it is a comfort, in a way, to know that they'll all outlast me.

FISH SAUSAGES

Here you have a perfect way to turn tattered loose ends of various fish into a delicacy. I've made these sausages with salmon, halibut, and flaky tails of various cheap white fish, adding in bits of seafood such as prawns, even bits of smoked salmon for extra flavour. If you don't have a steamer basket, the sausages can be poached in simmering water on the stovetop. Alternatively, you can forget casings altogether and roll the sausages in panko to be fried. For a quick sauce, steal the one from potato-crusted cod (p. 103), omitting the anchovies and substituting chives for the dill.

1-1/2 pounds (675 g) raw fish and seafood (2/3 halibut and 1/3 prawns works well)
4 slices white bread (about 4 ounces/110 g), crusts removed
2 egg whites
1/2 cup (125 mL) heavy cream
1-1/2 teaspoons Dijon mustard
1 tablespoon lemon juice
1/2 teaspoon paprika
Pinch cayenne pepper
Salt and black pepper
1-inch (2.5 cm) natural sausage casings (optional)

Cut the fish into chunks. Hold the bread under the hot tap, soak it through, then squeeze it out in your hands. Put both in a food processor with the egg whites, cream, mustard, lemon juice, paprika, and cayenne. Season well with salt and black pepper. Whiz until smooth, about a minute.

Pipe the mixture into sausage casings, tying them off at intervals. Alternatively, divide the mixture into 8 equal portions. (These will expand considerably during cooking, so, if you prefer, make 16 smaller versions.) Wrap each portion in plastic, rolling into a sausage shape and twisting the ends to secure. Refrigerate the sausages if you're not cooking them immediately.

Lay the sausages (in casings or plastic wrap) in a steamer basket, set it over simmering water in a wok, cover, and steam until cooked through, about 12 minutes.

Unwrap from the plastic wrap (no need if you've used proper casings) and serve.

MAKES: 8 SERVINGS

LOBSTER *with* RED LENTILS

Where I come from, lobster was long considered poor man's food. Such is certainly not the case in Paris, where one lobster alone can blow your entire food budget for the week. I was surprised, therefore, when a friend presented me with this clever lobster and red lentil number. The duo seem an unlikely pair, but here opposites attract: the lentils bring lobster down to earth and make a little bit go a long way, while the lobster lends an air of debonair to the dish. This has become one of my weeknight staples. Note that the fresh coriander leaves are an essential ingredient, adding as they do their wonderfully fragrant lightness.

2 tablespoons butter

1 small onion, minced

1/3 celery rib, very finely diced

1 small carrot, very finely diced

1 garlic clove, crushed

1/4 cup (60 mL) white wine

2 tablespoons tomato purée (not paste; optional)

1 cup (200 g) red lentils

2-1/2 cups (625 mL) fish stock or lobster broth

About 11 ounces (300 g) lobster meat, thawed if frozen

Salt and pepper

A few generous handfuls of fresh coriander leaves

Melt the butter in a medium saucepan. Add the onion, celery, and carrot. Gently fry until tender, about 10 minutes. Add the garlic and fry, stirring, for 1 minute. Pour in the wine and boil for a minute to reduce. Stir in the tomato purée (if using), then add the lentils and stock. Bring to a boil, reduce heat to a simmer, and cook until the lentils are starting to break down, about 15 minutes. The texture should be slightly soupy, not too, too dense.

Set aside 4 claws from the lobster meat and coarsely chop the rest. Stir all the meat, including the claws, into the lentils to warm through. Season with salt and pepper.

Ladle into warm soup plates, making sure there's a claw on top of each serving. Scatter over some of the coriander leaves and pass the remainder in a bowl for anyone who'd like more.

MAKES: 4 SERVINGS

CURRIED BLANQUETTE *of* SCALLOPS

A quick and comforting weeknight staple of mine is this light and healthy stew, which I serve in large soup plates for a proper main-course feel. Have a baguette on the side, if you like.

2 tablespoons butter

1 large onion, finely chopped

1 teaspoon curry powder, more to taste

1/8 teaspoon chili flakes

1 pound (450 g) waxy potatoes, peeled and diced

1/4 cup (60 mL) white wine

Salt and pepper

14 ounces (390 g) bay or sea scallops

6 ounces (170 g) spinach, trimmed and coarsely chopped

1/2 cup (125 mL) light cream

Heat the butter in a large saucepan and gently fry the onion for 5 minutes. Add the curry powder and chili flakes; cook, stirring, for 1 minute. Stir in the potatoes and wine. Bring to a boil. Pour in enough water to cover the potatoes by an inch (2.5 cm). Season with salt and pepper. Simmer until the potatoes are just shy of being tender, about 15 minutes.

Depending on the size of your scallops, cut them in half crosswise or quarter them lengthwise. (If they're the tiny ones, leave them whole.) Add them to the pot and simmer until just tender, about 5 minutes. Stir in the spinach and cook until wilted, about 2 minutes. Stir in the cream and heat through. Taste and adjust the seasonings and serve.

MAKES: 4 SERVINGS

SPRING CHICKEN *in a* PAN

. . . as opposed to *poule au pot*, or "chicken in a pot," the classic French poached chicken with spring vegetables in broth. This, instead, is a sort of sauté version made with breasts, which makes a fine weeknight dish for anyone who wants to eat a proper dinner of meat and vegetables but in a very simple and quick flavourful way.

1 pound (450 g) skin-on boneless chicken breasts (2 or 4, depending on size), halved

Salt and pepper

2 tablespoons butter

A drop of olive oil

2 garlic cloves, crushed

3 medium-small carrots (about 9 ounces/250 g), peeled and thinly sliced

3 medium-small leeks (about 9 ounces/250 g), trimmed and sliced

2 medium potatoes (about 9 ounces/250 g), peeled and thickly sliced

1/4 cup (60 mL) white wine

3/4 cup (175 mL) rich chicken stock

1 cup (150 g) fresh or frozen green peas

A handful of chopped fresh parsley and chives, or other herbs of your liking

Season the chicken with salt and pepper. Heat the butter and oil in a sauté pan over medium-high heat and brown the chicken, starting skin side down, 3 to 5 minutes per side. Remove to a plate. Reduce heat to medium-low. Add the garlic, carrots, and leeks to the pan, stir, then cover and sweat for 5 minutes.

Spread the potatoes over the vegetables, lay the chicken on top, and pour over the wine and stock. Cover and cook until everything is tender and the chicken is cooked through, 15 to 20 minutes, adding the peas for the last 2 minutes. Scatter over the herbs and serve from the sauté pan.

MAKES: 4 SERVINGS

Where Have All the Flowers Gone?

This will give you a little insight into the French psyche. I was at a neighbour's place for coffee one day and noticed that all the lovely flowers she used to have billowing out over the street in her window boxes had vanished. "Oh yes," she said with a tenor sigh. "Well, I could never get anyone to look after them properly when I went on holiday. I'd always come back to find them either brittle victims of drought or drowned in puddles." A pause . . . and then the truth came out.

"You know," she went on, "I used to get many compliments for my flowers. Oh yes! I'd look out all the time and catch passersby taking pictures of the window from below, cooing over how lovely it all looked. 'Oh charming!' they'd be saying. 'Isn't it *quaint!*' A real neighbourhood attraction! And then?

"Then, *that woman*"—a nod towards the street—"took the ground floor of the building across from me, installed a real estate agency, and put all those *horrible fluorescent signs* in all her windows to sell flats! *Quel horreur!* Well! Why should *she* get to stand in her doorway admiring the view of *my* place while I'm stuck up here staring down at her dump? *C'est injuste!* So I took all the flowers down, *ah oui! Ah, non, non, non, alors là non. Tu imagines?* She's not getting beautiful from me if she makes me look at ugly."

EXPATS' CHRISTMAS DINNER SALAD

There are holiday nights when you just want to stay quiet, but without losing the festive mood. That's where this recipe comes in. It's a chicken salad with jolly, Christmassy trimmings that feels as celebratory as a full-blown turkey dinner, but without the heavy commitment.

1 tablespoon butter
2 skinned cooked chicken breasts (about 1 pound/450 g)
2 blood oranges
1 teaspoon Dijon or grainy Dijon mustard
1 to 2 teaspoons red wine vinegar
1/4 cup (60 mL) olive oil
Salt and pepper
1/4 cup (60 mL) red currant jelly
A few handfuls of mâche or baby spinach
Several generous handfuls of fresh coriander leaves
A few handfuls of sliced almonds, lightly toasted
4 ounces (110 g) fresh chèvre, in pinches
A handful or two of pomegranate seeds

Melt the butter in a skillet and lightly brown the chicken breasts on both sides, a matter of minutes. Remove to a cutting board.

Zest 1 orange into a small bowl; set aside. Using a knife, cut the skin and pith off both oranges. Working over the zest bowl to catch the juice, cut between the membranes to remove the sections, placing the sections in a separate bowl.

Whisk the mustard into the zest and juice in the first bowl, then whisk in the vinegar and olive oil until blended. Season with salt and pepper. Finally, whisk in the jelly, allowing it to stay in small 3-D particles rather than dissolving completely.

Toss the mâche with the coriander leaves and arrange on a platter. Slice the chicken breasts and arrange over top. Scatter over the orange sections, almonds, chèvre, and pomegranate seeds. Evenly pour over the dressing, and serve.

MAKES: 4 SERVINGS

CHICKEN *and* ENDIVES
in CIDER SAUCE

The recipe for this delicate fall dish was given to me by a poultry man with an impressive stand at the fabulous Saint-Quentin market, not far from the Gare du Nord. I've often made it with guinea fowl, so feel free if you want to be more exotic. Browning the chicken and endives takes a bit of time, but it's effortless, and you are making a dinner-party-worthy one-pot dish here. Farro is a perfect side dish because of its wonderful bite and nuttiness, but a side dish isn't necessarily required at all. Put 2 cups (400 g) farro in a pot with 4 cups (1 L) water. Add salt, bring to a boil, cover, and simmer until tender but not bursting, about 30 minutes. Stir in a spoonful of butter, a big handful of finely chopped parsley, and a generous grinding of black pepper.

1 chicken or guinea fowl (about 3 pounds/1.35 kg), cut into 8 pieces	3 shallots, sliced
Salt and pepper	1 cup (250 mL) good-quality hard cider
1 tablespoon butter	1 cup (250 mL) chicken stock
6 endives (about 2 pounds/900 g), halved lengthwise	1 bay leaf
	1/4 cup (60 mL) heavy cream
	A handful of finely chopped fresh parsley

Season the chicken pieces with salt and pepper. Melt the butter in a heavy flameproof casserole or Dutch oven. When hot, brown the chicken, working in batches, until deeply golden on the skin side, about 4 minutes per side. Remove to a plate as you go.

Working again in batches, sauté the endives on the cut side for about 4 minutes, adding to the chicken as you go. Turn down the heat and gently sauté the shallots until soft, about 3 minutes.

Put the chicken and endives back in the casserole, pour over the cider and stock, and add the bay leaf. Bring to a simmer, cover, and cook until the chicken is tender, about 45 minutes.

Remove the chicken and endives to a serving dish and cover with foil to keep warm. Discard the bay leaf if you wish. Boil the cooking liquid down to sauce consistency, about 15 minutes. Whisk in the cream and boil down a bit longer if necessary to light sauce consistency. Taste and adjust the seasonings. Pour the sauce over the chicken. Sprinkle with parsley and serve.

MAKES: 6 SERVINGS

CHICKEN *and* ORANGE TAGINE

The list of ingredients is long, but they're mostly spices, and the prep time is next to nothing. The result is a sunny dish that's full of surprise and worthy of great company. If you're not a fan of fresh coriander, mint is fabulous here in its place. On the side you might like couscous with currants (p. 209).

4 organic thin-skinned oranges, washed

6 chicken legs, split if very large

1/4 cup (60 mL) olive oil

2 onions, sliced

2 teaspoons ground cumin

2 teaspoons ground coriander

1 teaspoon ground ginger

1 teaspoon turmeric

1/2 teaspoon cinnamon

Pinch saffron

A faint grating of nutmeg

4 garlic cloves, minced

A generous handful or two of finely chopped fresh parsley

1 cup (250 mL) orange juice

1 cup (250 mL) chicken stock

2 tablespoons sugar

Salt and pepper

1 cup (165 g) green olives, pitted if you prefer

Fresh coriander leaves or mint, for garnish

Cut each orange lengthwise into 8 wedges. Flick out any seeds.

At this point you can brown the chicken legs in oil and butter so that the skin looks good, or remove the skin from the chicken legs and proceed with the recipe.

Heat the oil in a Dutch oven and gently sauté the onions with the spices, stirring frequently, until soft, about 5 minutes. Add the garlic, parsley, orange juice, chicken stock, sugar, and salt and pepper to taste. Cover and simmer for half an hour. Remove the lid and continue simmering until the chicken is cooked through and the liquid has reduced to a nice sauce, about 20 minutes more.

Serve from the pot or in a warm serving dish, scattered with the olives and coriander.

MAKES: 6 SERVINGS

Candles

One day I looked up "candles" on the dreaded Wikipedia and got such a dull earful that I was put off buying candles for weeks. What I wanted was an expert opinion on what makes a truly great candle. I couldn't find any information I could trust, so now I'm desperate to meet a candle fanatic and pick their brains. What material makes the best candles, beeswax? Why do some burn down in about 30 seconds and destroy tabletops by melting into solid puddles, while others last endlessly and flicker soothingly rather than hysterically? Is there a reason for packaging candles in glass jars, as the luxury scented brands do? Speaking of scents, how is it that some candles release fragrances delicate and divine, while others act on the nostrils like the inside of a plastic-shoe factory? I throw my hands up! It's all a great mystery.

If I ever really set myself up permanently in the countryside somewhere (which would be heaven), I may try my hand at making my own candles. Meanwhile, I must navigate my way through life blindly buying candles and hoping for the best. I've learned it's no bargain to buy ultra-inexpensive candles, because for every one quality candle you buy you'll have to buy about 10 cheapos. A friend of mine swears by getting candles from some outfit that supplies cathedrals (apparently there are several around Saint-Sulpice). Original approach, although I'm not surprised: I have had good luck myself buying the odd candle from a monastery when driving through the countryside.

RÔTISSERIE CHICKEN DINNER

There's not a butcher shop in Paris that doesn't have a rôtisserie device outside, spinning chickens to golden perfection winter, spring, summer, and fall. If you've bought one to eat straightaway, obviously there's nothing to be done apart from carving, but if hours will pass before dinner, your chicken will need some reviving, which is a simple operation with this take-out-style approach: juicy chunks of chicken on a bed of crisp potato fingers with chewy garlic.

1 pound (450 g) oblong new potatoes, quartered lengthwise

Cloves from 1 head garlic, peeled and halved lengthwise

1 tablespoon olive oil

2 tablespoons butter

Salt and pepper

1 rôtisserie chicken (about 3 pounds/1.35 kg)

A generous handful of chopped fresh parsley

Heat the oven to 425°F (220°C). Put the potatoes and garlic on a baking sheet. Toss with the olive oil and spread in a single layer. Dot with the butter and season with salt and pepper. Roast for 20 minutes, tossing once halfway.

Meanwhile, dismantle the chicken by cutting it into 8 pieces. You can leave the bones in or not (but in any case save them for making stock later).

After the 20 minutes are up, toss the potatoes again, then lay the chicken pieces on top of the potatoes. Roast for another 10 minutes.

Spill the whole business onto a serving platter and scatter over the parsley before serving.

MAKES: 4 TO 6 SERVINGS

SEARED DUCK *with* PLUM COMPOTE

A very pretty dish for late summer. Serve with steamed green beans or a handful of watercress.

2 duck breasts (about 3/4 pound/340 g each)
1 pound (450 g) purple plums (about 6 medium), pitted
1/2 cup (125 mL) water
1/2 cup (125 mL) sugar
1 tablespoon grainy Dijon mustard
Salt and pepper

Score the duck breasts on the skin side (but do not cut into the meat) and set, skin side down, in a cold frying pan. Turn the heat to medium-low and render the fat, 5 to 10 minutes depending on how much fat there is, pouring off the fat as it melts. (Keep the fat for another use, such as roasting potatoes.)

While the fat renders, begin the compote. Cut each plum into 8 wedges, discarding the pits. Put in a saucepan with the water and sugar and simmer, stirring occasionally, until reduced to a chunky compote, about 20 minutes. Stir in the mustard. Season with salt and pepper.

Meanwhile, when the fat has rendered, remove the duck from the pan and pour off the fat. Increase the heat to medium-high, season the breasts with salt and pepper, and put them back in the pan, skin side down. Cook for about 7 minutes, then turn and cook for another 3 minutes or until done to your liking. Remove to a carving board to rest for 10 minutes. Carve and serve with the compote.

MAKES: 6 SERVINGS

ROSEMARY-MARINATED QUAIL

Quail must be the speediest of all birds to cook, and there's something about them that always feels like a treat. This is a herb-flavoured version, but they also like spice, so another time try them with a rub of crushed fennel, cumin, and coriander seeds. The farro on p. 121 would make a suitable side.

4 quail, split in half
Salt and pepper
3 to 4 tablespoons butter, softened
Leaves from 1 branch fresh rosemary, chopped
1 garlic clove, crushed

Season the quail with salt and pepper. Mix together the butter, rosemary, and garlic; rub it evenly over the quail and (carefully, so you don't tear the skin) as much under the skin as possible. If you have time, cover and refrigerate for an hour or longer to allow the flavours to infuse the birds.

Heat the broiler with the rack at the very top. Arrange the quail on a baking sheet skin side up and broil until the juices run clear, 12 to 15 minutes.

MAKES: 4 SERVINGS

CORDON BLEU CROQUETTES

These croquettes are embarrassingly retro, really, but fun to eat, and a great way to use up leftover cooked chicken. Crisp on the outside and creamy in the centre, they're a perfect answer for dinner when you tire of plain old chicken, or when you just want to feel like a kid again. You can also make croquettes with fish and/or seafood, the classic being grey shrimp, or *crevettes grises* (in which case a teaspoon or two of tomato paste might be added for flavour, and obviously the cheese and ham omitted).

For the croquette mixture
3 tablespoons (45 g) butter
1/4 cup (30 g) flour
1 cup (250 mL) milk
12 ounces (340 g) cooked chicken, shredded
6 ounces (170 g) ham, finely chopped
4 ounces (110 g) Gruyère, grated
1 tablespoon grated onion
1 tablespoon lemon juice
1/8 teaspoon cayenne pepper
1 tablespoon finely chopped fresh parsley
Salt and black pepper

For assembly
Flour, for dredging
1 egg, whisked with 1 teaspoon water,
    in a shallow bowl
Dry bread crumbs, for coating, on a plate
Peanut or grapeseed oil, for frying
Sprigs of fresh curly parsley, for garnish
Lemon wedges, for garnish

For the croquette mixture, melt the butter in a medium saucepan over medium heat. When the foaming subsides, after a minute or so, whisk in the flour and cook, whisking, for 1 minute. Whisk in the milk and continue whisking until the mixture is very thick, about 2 minutes. Remove from the heat.

Stir in the chicken, ham, cheese, onion, lemon juice, cayenne, and parsley. Season well with salt and black pepper. Transfer to a bowl, cover, and refrigerate until very stiff, about 2 hours.

To assemble the croquettes, flour a work surface. Flour your hands and shape the mixture into 12 balls, then roll into logs about 3 inches (7.5 cm) long, coating with flour as you go and shaking or brushing off the excess. Heat 2 inches (5 cm) oil in a large saucepan. The oil is ready when a rip of bread sizzles and starts to lightly colour. Working in batches, dip the floured croquettes first in the egg, then in bread crumbs to coat. Fry, turning with a slotted spoon at halftime, until all sides are browned, about 3 minutes total. The idea is to get the outsides nicely golden as the insides heat through. If the oil is too raging hot, the outside will crispen too quickly. Remove to paper towels to drain.

If you like, deep-fry some parsley sprigs for a few seconds until bright and crisp.

Arrange the croquettes on a warm serving platter, scatter over the deep-fried parsley sprigs, lay around some lemon wedges for squeezing, and serve.

MAKES: ABOUT 24 CROQUETTES

PANTRY DUCK PARMENTIER

Obviously, the fastest thing to do with store-bought confit duck legs is to blast them under the broiler for a few minutes to crispen the skin, then eat them. This recipe is more time-consuming, admittedly, but it is also a way to make four little duck legs serve eight easily—plus you can make it ahead of time and reheat just before serving. The same recipe is equally good with shredded leftover stewed lamb or beef.

4 confit duck legs

1 onion, chopped

2 shallots, minced

3 garlic cloves, crushed

1 tablespoon tomato paste

1/2 cup (125 mL) red wine

1 cup (250 mL) chicken or veal stock

1 cup (250 mL) tinned crushed tomatoes

2 bay leaves

A few pinches of piment d'Espelette or chili flakes

Salt and black pepper

1 pound (450 g) Yukon Gold or other floury potatoes, peeled

1/4 cup (55 g) butter, cut into small cubes

3/4 cup (175 mL) warm milk

A squirt of truffle paste (optional)

2 tablespoons finely grated Parmesan cheese

Fresh chervil, for garnish

Scrape the fat from the duck legs. Keep a spoonful, and reserve the rest for another use (such as frying potatoes). Carefully remove the skin from the duck legs and lay it right side up on a baking sheet; set aside. Shred the meat with a knife or with two forks and set aside.

Heat the spoonful of duck fat in an ovenproof sauté pan or cast-iron frying pan and gently fry the onion and shallots until very soft, about 10 minutes. Add the garlic and fry, stirring frequently, for 1 minute. Stir in the tomato paste, then add the wine, chicken stock, tomatoes, bay leaves, piment d'Espelette, and duck meat. Simmer, uncovered, until you've achieved a thick sauce, about 20 minutes. Season with salt if necessary and with black pepper. (*Recipe continues . . .*)

While the duck simmers, heat the oven to 375°F (190°C). Boil the potatoes in a pot of salted water until tender.

When the oven is hot, pop in the duck skin and bake, pouring off the fat occasionally as it renders, until crisp and golden, about 15 minutes. Pat dry with paper towels, chop coarsely, and transfer to a small serving bowl. Set aside.

Drain the potatoes. Peel and mash with the butter, milk, and truffle paste (if using). Season with salt and pepper. When the duck is ready, spread the potatoes evenly over top. Scatter over the Parmesan cheese and a little more piment d'Espelette if you like. Bake until the potatoes are bubbly and beginning to brown, about 20 minutes. Scatter over the chervil and serve straight from the pan, with the crackling on the side.

MAKES: 8 SERVINGS

BAVETTE *with* HERB BUTTER

Topping a steak with a round of flavoured butter is a classic method, but it's not seen all that often anymore. I love a combination of parsley and tarragon in the butter; in fact it almost tricks your mouth into thinking you're eating béarnaise sauce. If you're flush, feel free to use a more expensive cut, such as tournedos.

1/4 cup (55 g) butter, at room temperature
2 tablespoons finely chopped fresh tarragon
1 tablespoon finely chopped fresh parsley
Pinch cayenne pepper
2 to 3 teaspoons of olive oil
1-1/2 pounds (675 g) bavette steak
Lemon wedges, for garnish

Put the butter in a bowl. Add the herbs and cayenne; knead to mix thoroughly. Wrap in plastic wrap and roll to shape into a log. Refrigerate until firm, about an hour.

Heat the oil in a heavy frying pan over medium-high heat and fry the steak on both sides to your liking—for me, that's about 4 to 6 minutes per side for medium-rare. Remove to a carving board to rest for about 5 minutes.

Slice the log of butter into fat rounds. Slice the steak against the grain and arrange on a platter. Top with coins of butter, garnish with lemon wedges, and serve.

MAKES: 4 SERVINGS

STEAK TARTARE

Burgers are storming Paris at the moment—*hélas!*—and everyone eats them with a knife and fork. But steak tartare remains a bistro favourite, and I prefer it hands down, as long as it's a good one, which, quite frankly, is a rare find (no pun intended). To make your own, be sure to get the meat from a reputable butcher and let him know you'll be serving it raw. A bit of fresh horseradish grated over the final product is classic. The contrasting crunch of thin slices of lightly toasted olive-oil-rubbed baguette are *de rigueur* with this, unless you're going to play bistro yourself and serve it with crisp french fries.

8 ounces (225 g) rib-eye steak

1/2 shallot, minced

2 anchovies, rinsed and chopped

1 raw egg yolk (or 1 teaspoon mayonnaise)

A handful of chopped fresh parsley

1 tablespoon chopped cornichons

1 teaspoon chopped capers

2 teaspoons Dijon mustard

2 teaspoons Worcestershire sauce

2 teaspoons Cognac (optional)

A few drops of hot pepper sauce

Salt and pepper

A squeeze of lemon juice

A handful of micro-greens, for garnish

Olive oil

Make this dish just before serving.

If you haven't had the butcher mince the meat for you, put it in the freezer for about 30 minutes to make it easier to cut, then mince it very, very finely with a knife.

In a large bowl, mix together the shallot, anchovies, egg yolk, parsley, cornichons, capers, mustard, Worcestershire sauce, Cognac (if using), and hot pepper sauce. Add the meat and mix well. Season with salt, pepper, and lemon juice. Shape into 4 patties and arrange on plates.

For garnish, dress a handful of micro-greens very lightly with olive oil, lemon juice, and salt and pepper. Set a pinch on top of each tartare shape and serve.

MAKES: 4 SERVINGS

BEAUTIFUL CÔTE *de* BOEUF

Depending where you live, you may have to ask your butcher to prepare this cut for you, which will enhance your relationship tenfold, since butchers love getting special requests from adoring clients. It's basically a slice of rib roast, fat, thick, and succulent, still on the bone. It tastes out of this world and looks extremely impressive, especially when the rib bone is left on, Flintstone-style (rather than hacked off by the well-meaning butcher who prepared my cut for the photo on p. 138. I didn't have the heart to tell him). It's also expensive, so be prepared, but it's a perfect choice for when you need to produce a celebratory feast in under an hour. Delicious with whole baked celeriac (p. 178) and a lightly dressed watercress salad afterwards to soak up the juices. I like this with horseradish sauce.

1 bone-in côte de boeuf (about 3 pounds/1.35 kg)
1 teaspoon olive oil
Salt and pepper
2 tablespoons butter
1 head garlic, broken into unpeeled cloves
A handful of finely chopped fresh parsley

Turn your oven on full blast with the rack one-third of the way down from the top. Rub the beef with the olive oil and set it in a small roasting pan. Season with pepper.

When the oven is up to full heat, roast the meat for 10 minutes. Turn, throw the butter and garlic into the pan, and roast for a further 10 minutes for medium-rare.

Remove from the oven, throw over the parsley, and season with salt. Tent with foil and let rest for 15 to 20 minutes.

Carve the meat against the grain into thin slices at the table and serve with the pan juices spooned over.

MAKES: 6 SERVINGS

VIENNESE VEAL CUTLET

Amazing the responses you get when you corner people and ask what their staple, once-a-week dinner dish is. *Escalope de veau panée* was one of the lesser-expected revelations of a friend of mine, not only because I don't think of veal as an everyday sort of meat but also because this particular take on it is so Vienna. (Mind you, every butcher in Paris sells breaded escalopes ready to fry, so it's legit.) I decided to try it myself one day and I could immediately see why it had become my friend's staple: tender and juicy on the inside, crisp on the outside, perked up with a squirt of lemon . . . Almost makes you feel as though you could run your own Austrian Empire!

4 thin veal escalopes (about 4 ounces/110 g each), cut in half crosswise

Salt and pepper

About 2 tablespoons butter

About 2 tablespoons olive oil

Flour, for dredging, on a plate

1 egg, lightly beaten, in a shallow dish

Fresh bread crumbs (p. 207), for dredging, on a plate

2 tablespoons capers

A handful of chopped fresh parsley

4 lemon wedges

Pound the veal lightly with a meat mallet a few times to flatten slightly, then season with salt and pepper.

Heat the butter and oil in a large frying pan over medium-high heat. When the fat is sizzling, working in batches, dip each escalope first in flour, shaking off the excess, then in egg, letting excess drip off, then in the bread crumbs to coat both sides. Fry until golden on the underside, 2 to 3 minutes. Flip and fry until golden. Remove the cutlets to a warm serving platter.

Add the capers to the pan and fry for a few seconds. Scatter over the parsley, then pour the pan juices over the cutlets. Serve with lemon wedges.

MAKES: 4 SERVINGS

FORK *and* SPOON LAMB
with MINTY YOGURT SAUCE

Slow cooking can often be much less effortful than last-minute, speedy preparations, so that's why I pull out this recipe when I'm feeling overwhelmed. It's so easy it almost hurts, and people rave at the results. Serve, if you can, with potatoes roasted in duck fat (p. 203) so they're nice and crisp. You can do the potatoes once the lamb is out of the oven. They'll take about 45 minutes and the lamb, wrapped in foil, can easily sit that long on the countertop and still stay nice and warm.

For the lamb
1 bone-in lamb shoulder (about 4 pounds/1.8 kg)
Salt and pepper
2 heads garlic, broken into unpeeled cloves
About 2 tablespoons olive oil
1/2 cup (125 mL) white wine

For the sauce
1-1/2 cups (375 mL) plain yogurt
Leaves from a bunch of fresh mint
1 garlic clove, crushed
Zest of 1 lemon
Salt and pepper

Heat the oven to 350°F (180°C). Set a piece of foil large enough to wrap the lamb in a baking pan. Fold up the sides a little. Season the lamb with salt and pepper and lay it on the foil. Scatter the garlic around, drizzle over the oil, pour in the wine, and wrap to seal tightly. Bake until the meat is fork-tender (which means, basically, falling from the bone), about 4 hours.

For the sauce, stir together the yogurt, mint, garlic, and lemon zest. Season to taste with salt and pepper. Transfer to a serving bowl, cover, and refrigerate until serving.

If you're not serving the lamb right away, just leave it in the foil and it will retain its heat for about an hour. To serve, unwrap it and set it on a platter with a large fork and spoon as serving implements. Pass, with the sauce close on its heels.

MAKES: 6 SERVINGS

Edible Windowsills

The idea of gardening in Paris is a bit of a long shot, but lots of people nonetheless like to grow a few little things on their kitchen windowsills. My friend Camille's windowsill in the 11th arrondissement boasts an inspiring display of watercress, basil, and a tomato vine. So, clearly, it can be done! All you need is a little bit of dirt and a few seedlings. Camille tells me that the best windowsill trick is green garlic. Say you have an old garlic clove with a sizable green sprout in it. Just place it, peeled, in a small pot of earth, germ pointing skywards, and it will grow in no time at all. Clip the green bit as it grows and chop it to put in salads. Children love the magic of this sort of thing when they do what I call "the eggshell man." Simply wet a piece of paper towel and stuff it into half an eggshell, which you've set in an egg cup. Scatter a few lentils onto the towel and draw a happy face on the eggshell. In a few days, the lentils will sprout and your little man will have hair!

VEAL FRICASSÉE *with* MUSHROOMS

Here's an ideal dinner-party dish, easily doable even on a weeknight because the shopping is minimal. It's not a five-minute deal, but it is low-maintenance. While the stew simmers, gossip over a glass of wine and a few green olives. Serve the stew with roasted pumpkin wedges with rosemary (p. 193) on the side and follow up with a green salad.

About 1/4 cup (60 mL) olive oil

1/4 cup (55 g) butter

3 pounds (1.35 kg) veal shoulder, cut into 1-inch (2.5 cm) pieces

Salt and pepper

2 medium onions, sliced

1 tablespoon flour

1 cup (250 mL) white wine

1-1/2 cups (375 mL) chicken stock

2 bay leaves

2 pounds (900 g) mixed mushrooms, such as chanterelles, porcini, cremini, and black trumpet, sliced or quartered if large

2 garlic cloves, minced

Chopped fresh parsley, for garnish

Heat a spoonful each of the oil and butter in a heavy flameproof casserole or Dutch oven. Season the veal generously with salt and pepper. Working in batches, fry the veal on all sides until well browned, removing from the pan as you go, about 20 minutes total. (You may need to add more fat to the pan between batches.)

When all the meat is browned, reduce the heat to medium. Add another spoonful each of oil and butter and gently fry the onions until soft and lightly golden, about 5 minutes, stirring in the flour for a minute at the end. Put the veal back in the pan and add the wine, stock, and bay leaves. Bring to a boil, cover, reduce the heat, and simmer gently until fork-tender, about an hour. Remove the lid and continue simmering for another half-hour to reduce the juices.

While the veal simmers, prepare the mushrooms. Heat a spoonful each of oil and butter in a large sauté pan or wok over medium-high heat until sizzling. Working in batches if necessary, fry the mushrooms until tender, about 5 minutes, removing to a bowl as cooked. Add the garlic with the last batch. Combine all the mushrooms and season with salt and pepper.

Transfer the veal to a large serving dish and scatter over the mushrooms and parsley. Serve.

MAKES: 6 TO 8 SERVINGS

The SPEEDIEST of LAMB CHOPS

I love this method of preparing chops: you just lay them all on a baking sheet, wave them under the broiler, and presto, they're ready to serve without any carving required.

12 small lamb chops (about 2 ounces/55 g each)
Olive oil
Salt and black pepper
Pinch cayenne pepper, or a few drops of Worcestershire sauce

Heat the broiler. Rub the chops with olive oil on both sides and lay on a baking sheet. Season with salt, black pepper, and cayenne (or Worcestershire sauce, if you're an Anglo expat). Broil for 3 minutes per side. Turn off the oven and let rest for 5 minutes, with the oven door open, before serving.

MAKES: 4 SERVINGS

CHOUCROUTE GARNIE *à la* ME

It's Strasbourg that's famous for choucroute garnie, but Parisians love it, too, in the cold months. It's a warming, convivial dish that feels like a proper feast, which may explain why one friend once served it on New Year's Eve. I leave out the traditional pork hocks here, which saves a good deal of time. Bacon flavours the sauerkraut, then how you cobble together your sausage selection will depend on where you live. In Paris, I buy a Montbéliard, a saucisse fumée (smoked sausage), a saucisse à l'ail (garlic sausage), and a few frankfurters. Elsewhere, a combination of frankfurters, kielbasa, and knockwurst is an alternative. Serve with 2 pounds (900 g) peeled potatoes, boiled and tossed in butter and parsley.

2 bay leaves

8 juniper berries

6 whole cloves

1/2 teaspoon black peppercorns

2 tablespoons duck fat

1 slab smoked bacon (7 ounces/200 g),
    cut into chunks

1 large onion, chopped

2 garlic cloves, minced

2 firm apples, peeled, cored, and chopped

2 pounds (900 g) store-bought sauerkraut,
    rinsed and drained

2 cups (500 mL) dry Riesling or ale

2 pounds (900 g) assorted sausages
    (see headnote)

Heat the oven to 350°F (180°C). Wrap the bay leaves, juniper berries, cloves, and peppercorns in a square of cheesecloth. Tie to secure and set aside.

Heat the duck fat in a Dutch oven and fry the bacon until cooked but not crisping. Remove the bacon and set aside. Add the onion to the pot and cook until soft, about 8 minutes. Stir in the garlic and apples; cook for a minute. Return the bacon to the pan along with the sauerkraut. Pour over the wine, then tuck in the cheesecloth of flavourings. Bring to a simmer, cover, and simmer for 30 minutes. Nestle the sausages in the sauerkraut (unless you prefer to boil them separately), cover, and transfer to the oven for an hour.

Transfer the sausages to a cutting board and slice or cut into chunks, depending on the sausage. Arrange the sauerkraut on a large warm platter. Arrange the sausages on top. Serve with boiled potatoes and an assortment of mustards.

MAKES: 8 SERVINGS

PORK ROAST *with* MUSTARD SAUCE

If you really want to cook fast-fast, you can use a couple of pork tenderloins instead of a roast, but I prefer something with a bit more fat so the meat stays juicy and has some proper taste. Of course, the whole business can be done on the stovetop if you use pork chops, but I think if you're serving more than two people, a roast is simplest. A nice side dish is simply chard sautéed with garlic.

1 boneless pork roast (about 2 pounds/900 g)
Salt and pepper
1 tablespoon fat or olive oil
A handful of chopped fresh thyme
4 to 6 tablespoons Dijon mustard
1 onion, finely chopped
1/2 cup (125 mL) white wine
1/2 cup (125 mL) chicken stock
1/4 cup (60 mL) heavy cream
A handful of chopped fresh parsley, for garnish

Heat the oven to 350°F (180°C). Season the roast with salt and pepper. Heat the fat in a sauté pan over medium-high heat and brown the meat well on all sides, 3 to 4 minutes per side. Transfer the roast to a baking dish or roasting pan. Mix together the thyme and mustard and rub it all over the pork. In the same sauté pan, adding a bit more fat if needed, fry the onion until soft, 5 to 7 minutes. Scatter the onion around the pork. Deglaze the pan with the wine, then pour it around the pork. Pour in the stock.

Roast until cooked to your liking—for me, that's about 160°F (70°C) on the meat thermometer, 45 minutes to an hour, for meat that is just cooked through with the faintest hint of pink.

Remove the roast to a carving board. Whisk the cream into the pan juices. Bring to a boil, reducing to sauce consistency if necessary. Taste and adjust the seasonings.

Carve the meat into thin slices and arrange on a serving platter. Pour over the sauce, sprinkle with parsley, and serve.

MAKES: 6 SERVINGS

Storing *Fines Herbes*

One distinguishing feature of French cooking must certainly be the liberal use of fresh herbs. They're readily available at every greengrocer and should always be at hand, because they're often key to turning an otherwise dull dish into a master-piece. Personally, I'd be non-functional in a kitchen without them.

Most herbs are, of course, extremely delicate and not overly long-lasting in their fresh state. Bay leaves, rosemary, summer savory, and thyme are exceptions. These you can tie with string and hang decoratively in the kitchen to dry; they cozy a place up instantly and make it feel ready for action.

The best way to keep in shape the leafier varieties, such as parsley, coriander, basil, dill, tarragon, sage, and mint, is to wrap them in damp paper towel and store them in plastic bags in the fridge. It's especially critical to apply this approach to chervil, which seems the most fragile and fleeting of the lot: like a field poppy, once picked, it will faint like a shocked Victorian lady right into your hand.

GYPSY PORK BOULETTES

Sounds like a gambling machine . . . It's not, obviously, but even if it were, it would be the gambling machine on which you always win. The English translation of *boulettes* is "meatballs," but these are more like patties the shape of UFOs, and are fried, not plunged into a sauce to simmer. These come via a Romanian-Parisian friend. Similar versions abound in Scandinavia, using thyme sometimes instead of dill, or even using 1/2 cup (60 g) flour (or, scandal of scandals, dehydrated potato powder) to replace the potato. Serve the boulettes with School Night Potato Purée on p. 202.

For the boulettes
1-1/2 pounds (675 g) ground pork
1 large onion, very, very finely minced, or grated
3 to 4 garlic cloves, grated
1 medium potato (any kind), peeled and grated
Leaves from 1/2 bunch of fresh parsley, chopped
Fronds from 1 bunch of fresh dill, chopped
2 eggs, lightly beaten
Salt and pepper

For frying
About 1 cup (125 g) flour, for shaping
Peanut oil, for frying

For the boulettes, put all the ingredients in a big bowl and squish them around with your hands to mix thoroughly. Shape into 1/4-cup (60 mL) balls. (You can make them ahead to this point. Cover and refrigerate.) Just before cooking, put the flour onto a plate and season with salt (you'll want about 2 teaspoons) and pepper. Flatten the boulettes between your palms into UFO-style patties (slightly sloping down at the edges), then coat them in the flour.

In a large sauté pan, heat a good 3/4 inch (2 cm) oil over medium-high heat. You want it hot enough to gently sizzle a rip of bread but not at so raging a bubble that it risks cooking the outside of the boulettes in a flash whilst leaving the insides raw. When the oil is hot, lay in as many boulettes as you can fit without overcrowding and fry on both sides until wonderfully golden and cooked through, about 7 minutes total.

Remove the boulettes to a warm platter as you go and cover loosely with foil to keep warm. Serve.

MAKES: 6 SERVINGS

ISHES

SIDE DISHES

Butter-Braised Lettuce 158

Endives in Orange Butter 159

Pea Timbales 163

Summer Vegetables en Papillote 164

Zucchini Stewed in Olive Oil 165

Tomato Orbs with Thyme 168

Roasted Haricots Verts with Garlic and Mint 169

Carrots under Parchment 172

Baby Bok Choy with Chorizo 173

Wilted Spinach with Oranges 175

Whole Baked Celeriac 178

Alabaster Eggplant Compote 179

Roasted Confetti Ratatouille 181

Deep-Fried Broccoli with Hazelnut Mayonnaise 182

Roasted Cauliflower with Lentils and Capers 183

Fennel Gratin 186

Glazed Pearl Onions with Sage 187

Beet "Gratin" 189

Potiron Pumpkin Wedges with Rosemary 193

Turnips in Miso Butter 194

Cocotte of Winter Vegetables with Crème Fraîche 195

Apple and Red Onion Compote 197

Fondant Garlic Butter Potatoes 198

Crushed New Potatoes with Black Olives and Cherry Tomatoes 199

School Night Potato Purée 202

Duck Fat Potatoes 203

Two-Potato Gratin 204

Egg Noodles with Green Peppercorns 208

Couscous with Currants 209

Burnt Angel Hair with Green Onions 211

Riz au Lit 212

Beer and Buckwheat Crêpes 213

Polenta with Blue Cheese en Terrine 214

BUTTER-BRAISED LETTUCE

Little Gems are the lettuce you find in Paris, but butter lettuce, split in half or quartered, also works, as long as you belt it around the middle with a piece of string to keep it intact. The result will be a light and delicious accompaniment to fish or fowl.

4 Little Gems, halved
2 tablespoons butter
1/4 cup (60 mL) veal or beef stock
Salt and pepper

Blanch the lettuce in boiling salted water for 30 seconds, then drain and immediately shock in ice-cold water. Drain again and squeeze dry in a tea towel.

Melt the butter in a sauté pan over medium-high heat. Add the lettuce, cover, and cook, turning occasionally, until tender, about 5 minutes. Pour over the stock and reduce, a matter of minutes. Season with salt and pepper. Serve.

MAKES: 4 SERVINGS

ENDIVES *in* ORANGE BUTTER

Endives are decadent when cooked to ultra softness in brown butter. They get a bit candied, which their slightly bitter edge adores. Delicious with fish or pork.

2 tablespoons butter
6 endives (about 2 pounds/900 g), halved lengthwise and trimmed
Juice of 1/2 orange
2 tablespoons water
Salt and pepper

Melt the butter over medium-high heat in a sauté pan large enough to hold the endives in a single layer. Lay in the endives cut side down and brown well, about 5 minutes. When caramelized on the underside, add the juice and water and season with salt and pepper. Cover with a piece of parchment and tuck it down the sides of the pan. Cook over low heat until the endives are tender, about 5 minutes. Serve.

MAKES: 6 SERVINGS

PEA TIMBALES

These adorable little flans are a quick way to turn virtually any vegetable into the epitome of elegance. If you're replacing the peas with, say, corn, squash, asparagus, carrot, fennel, or parsnip—whatever your little heart dreams up—know that for the recipe below, you will need about 1 cup (250 mL) of puréed cooked vegetable. You may want to omit the mint, depending on what veg you're using. The water bath is optional: a water bath will give you a creamy texture, whereas no water bath will result in a slightly firmer flan. Both are good. These are splendid with lamb or chicken.

2 cups (300 g) cooked green peas
1 garlic clove
About 6 large fresh mint leaves, shredded
1/2 cup (125 mL) chicken or vegetable stock or water
1/4 cup (10 g) finely grated Parmesan cheese
3 eggs
1/2 cup (125 mL) heavy cream
Salt and pepper

Heat the oven to 350°F (180°C). Line the bottoms of 6 buttered 1/2-cup (125 mL) ramekins with rounds of parchment. If you're using a water bath, set the ramekins in a baking pan and bring a kettle of water to a boil. If not using a water bath, simply set them on a baking sheet.

Purée the peas with the garlic, mint, stock, and Parmesan cheese in a blender until very smooth. Add the eggs and cream; pulse to blend. Season with salt and pepper. Pour into the ramekins.

If using a water bath, set the pan of ramekins in the oven, then pour the boiled water in around them to come halfway up their sides. Either way, bake until set, about 30 minutes. Cool at least 10 minutes before unmoulding onto a platter. These are equally good warm or at room temperature.

MAKES: 6 SERVINGS

SUMMER VEGETABLES *en* PAPILLOTE

There's something about baking in paper that's fun. Here, for example, we have not just another baking sheet of vegetables and herbs but an envelope of goodies that have at once baked and steamed together, only to land before us in an enticing paper package. (Why, it's like getting mail from a cherished aunt travelling abroad!) Do experiment with different vegetable combinations, depending on what you find in the crisper. This is nice to serve with meat, fish, or fowl off the grill.

About 12 cherry tomatoes on the vine

1 cup (200 g) shelled fava beans (frozen is fine)

1 small zucchini (5 ounces/140 g), sliced

A head of garlic, broken into unpeeled cloves

A generous drizzling of olive oil

A few sprigs of fresh thyme

1 branch fresh rosemary, cut into 4 pieces

Salt and pepper

Heat the oven to 400°F (200°C). Cut a large piece of parchment paper and lay the vegetables and garlic on one half of it. Drizzle with olive oil, scatter over the herbs, and season with salt and pepper. Toss gently with your hands once or twice.

Fold the paper over top, like a letter. Starting at one end, fold and twist the edges to seal the contents completely. (This is important. You want to seal all the cooking juices and vapours inside. If you're worried, you can do like my friend Nathalie, who folds and staples her papillotes!)

Lay the package on a baking sheet and bake for 45 minutes, by which time the vegetables will cooked and crinkled (heading on their way to confit, even). Slide the paper package onto a serving platter and carry it to the table. Cut a giant X into the top with scissors to open it up, and serve immediately, straight out of the paper.

MAKES: 2 SERVINGS

ZUCCHINI STEWED *in* OLIVE OIL

Utter simplicity to make and tasting of virtue. I have a friend who eats heaps of this all on its own for lunch.

2 small zucchini (about 5 ounces/140 g each), cut into chunks
2 garlic cloves, sliced
A palmful of fresh thyme leaves
1/4 cup (60 mL) olive oil
Salt and pepper
Grated Parmesan cheese, for serving

Put the zucchini, garlic, thyme, and oil in a medium saucepan. Season with salt and pepper, cover, bring to a simmer, and cook, stirring once or twice, until done to your liking. The zucchini will be tender in under 5 minutes. Serve, passing grated Parmesan cheese for anyone who'd like it sprinkled over.

MAKES: 4 SERVINGS

TOMATO ORBS *with* THYME

A variety of medium-to-small heirloom tomatoes in various colours will give the most beautiful result here, but I also make the dish with even-sized red tomatoes and diners are very pleased. This is perfect as a side dish to grilled meats, but also lovely sopped up with baguette as a first course.

1-1/2 pounds (675 g) heirloom tomatoes
1/2 cup (125 mL) tomato purée
3 garlic cloves, sliced
Salt and pepper
1 bunch of fresh thyme
2 tablespoons olive oil

Heat the oven to 400°F (200°C). Bring a large pot of water to a boil.

With a sharp knife, score an X in the bottom of each tomato and drop them into the boiling water until the skins start to loosen, about 15 seconds. Remove to ice-cold water to shock them, then peel. Set the tomatoes in a baking dish.

Pour the tomato purée around the whole tomatoes. Scatter over the garlic and season with salt and pepper. Tuck the thyme sprigs in and around, then drizzle over the olive oil.

Bake until slumpy soft and intensified, 30 to 45 minutes, depending on the size and ripeness of the tomatoes. Serve warm or at room temperature.

MAKES: 6 TO 8 SERVINGS

ROASTED HARICOTS VERTS
with GARLIC and MINT

Even the mint gets roasted, and it still keeps its zing, which is a great foil to the density of the garlic. For best results, use haricots verts—slender green beans—rather than the woody fat ones.

1 pound (450 g) thin green beans, trimmed
8 garlic cloves, peeled and quartered lengthwise
About 20 fresh mint leaves, torn
2 to 3 tablespoons olive oil
Salt and pepper

Heat the oven to 375°F (190°C). Toss all the ingredients together on a baking sheet, then spread out in a single layer. Bake, without stirring, until the green beans are slightly shrivelled and starting to crispen, about 20 minutes. Serve.

MAKES: 4 SERVINGS

The Good Side of Greed

Parisians have only the tiniest freezer space, usually no more that the little section at the top of their refrigerators, so it's not possible to store very much. However, a few things are so precious it would be madness not to keep space for them. Whenever you fry or roast meat, for example, and are not using the juices, the pan should be deglazed and the juices saved, even if it's only enough to fill a single cube in an ice tray. For instance, just the other day I roasted a leg of lamb and, wanting a more substantial sauce than what the lamb yielded, I added a cube of juices left over from another night's steaks. Perfect! Chicken bones are also crucial to hang on to. Usually I make stock from them immediately, but if I don't have time, I freeze them until I'm ready for risotto. And the last thing, which perhaps it sounds absurd to save, but isn't, are any waters that high-quality vegetables have boiled in. Obviously, it's impossible to save them all, but at least if I know I have a soup coming up, I'll stash away a cup or two of potato water or squash water to add for extra flavour. All this sounds like the practice of a miser, but in fact it's one motivated by sheer greed. For taste, will save!

CARROTS *under* PARCHMENT

This cooking method is popular among chefs. The carrots, which taste ultra-carroty, keep their shape and become completely imbued with butter.

1-1/2 pounds (675 g) carrots, peeled
1/4 cup (55 g) butter
Salt

Leave the carrots whole or halve them lengthwise, depending on their thickness. You can also cut them into thick coins.

Melt the butter in a large sauté pan. Add the carrots and season with salt. Cover with a round of parchment cut slightly larger than the pan and tuck it down around the edges of the carrots like a blanket.

Cook over low heat until the carrots are soft all the way through, 15 to 30 minutes, depending how you've cut them. Serve.

MAKES: 6 SERVINGS

BABY BOK CHOY *with* CHORIZO

Bok choy is an elegant-looking vegetable, but when served whole, as it so often is, I never find it easy to eat. Here is a European treatment, as gorgeous as it is good for you. Feel free to replace the chorizo with bacon, cut into squares before frying.

4 baby bok choy
1 tablespoon olive oil
About 2 inches (5 cm) cured chorizo, very thinly sliced
2 tablespoons butter
Salt and pepper

Cut the bok choy between the white and green and set the greens aside. Quarter the white stems lengthwise, removing the core, so you have a pile of roughly 1-inch (2.5 cm) white squares.

Heat the oil in a sauté pan over medium-high heat. Either leave the chorizo in rounds or slice the rounds into matchsticks, then fry for about 20 seconds. Remove to a small dish.

Melt the butter in the pan, then add the bok choy stems. Cook until tender, about 5 minutes, stirring occasionally, then add the leaves, tossing to wilt, about a minute longer. Put the chorizo back in and season with salt (only if needed) and pepper. Tumble onto a platter and serve.

MAKES: 4 SERVINGS

WILTED SPINACH *with* ORANGES

The simple addition of acidic orange sections gives dark spinach a nice bit of perking up. I prefer them in segments, but if you're in a wheely mood, feel free to do them in slices as in the picture opposite. This is best made with nice big flags of robust spinach leaves, which hold their shape. If you're dealing with less stout spinach that wilts to nothing when cooked, you may need to increase quantities.

2 oranges
2 tablespoons butter
8 ounces (225 g) spinach
Salt and pepper

Remove the skins and pith from the oranges with a sharp knife. Cut the sections from between the membranes and place them in a bowl, flicking out any seeds as you go. Squeeze the juice into a glass and drink it.

Melt the butter in a sauté pan. Add the spinach leaves and cover to wilt just slightly. Do not reduce to a purée. Stir in the orange sections. Season with salt and pepper. Serve.

MAKES: 4 SERVINGS

Heavenly Hosting

"The best hosts put a thread of informality through everything," a friend of mine observed. "It's the feeling they create that differentiates them more than the food, or the setting."

Now, "informality" isn't the sort of word that springs into most people's minds when they think of Paris, but it's true. Dinner plans are made very spontaneously, people generally arrive on foot, and Parisians so much associate the dinner hour with relaxing and shedding the woes of the day that informality is almost automatic. Even formally set tables can be the scene of informal dining, because the mood is somehow right. This makes it easy on hosts, in a way, but of course it's the host's responsibility to set the tone in the first place.

I remember one dinner years ago in the 7th arrondissement in a rather elaborate apartment. I didn't know the host and I was slightly intimidated when I walked in because the table was set in a very grand manner indeed. I half expected Escoffier to appear, hired from "the other side" to do the catering. But it wasn't like that at all. The hostess had cooked the meal herself. When we sat down, she brought out a platter of salmon, a bowl of boiled potatoes, and a small bottle of prized olive oil, which she passed along with fleur de sel as the only adornments. I suppose there must have been a green salad and cheese after that, and then a thin chocolate cake, which in fact she hadn't made . . . but her grandmother had. I can't say it was the most creative meal I've ever partaken of, but as far as being unpretentious goes, it gets full marks.

WHOLE BAKED CELERIAC

This may take a while to bake, but you'd be hard pressed to find a recipe that requires less effort. The result is celery root impossibly fragrant and intense in taste, impressive to look at, and easy to serve. I like it with roast beef dripping in meaty juices or with Beautiful Côte de Boeuf (p. 139).

1/2 lemon
1 celeriac bulb (about 1 pound/450 g)
1 tablespoon olive oil
Salt and pepper

Heat the oven to 400°F (200°C). Finely grate the lemon zest; set aside the zest and keep the lemon half.

Peel the celeriac using a sharp knife, then rub it all over with the cut side of the lemon. Set the celeriac on a piece of foil large enough to wrap it. Now rub it all over with olive oil, salt, pepper, and the lemon zest. Wrap to seal, place in a baking pan, and bake until soft (unwrap slightly and test with a knife), about an hour. Keep the celeriac wrapped in foil until serving. (It will stay warm for up to an hour.)

Unwrap at the table, letting the steam rise up out of the package. Cut into wedges to serve.

MAKES: 6 SERVINGS

ALABASTER EGGPLANT COMPOTE

By removing the skin from eggplant, you practically discover a whole new vegetable, melt-in-the-mouth buttery in texture and with a fine alabaster sculptural look that makes you want to consider selling it off at an exorbitant price to Sotheby's. Mellow, golden, creamy, mild: perfect with lamb chops (p. 147).

2 pounds (900 g) eggplant, peeled
Salt and pepper
A few tablespoons of olive oil
2 tablespoons butter
A handful of coarsely chopped fresh parsley, mint, or coriander

Cut the eggplant into large chunks and season with salt. Heat the oil and butter in a sauté pan over medium-high heat. Add the eggplant and cook, stirring often, until lightly golden, about 5 minutes. Pour over 1/2 cup (125 mL) water, cover, reduce the heat, and simmer until tender, about 20 minutes. If any water remains, remove the lid and continue cooking to evaporate it.

Add the butter and stir through to melt. Toss in the parsley, season with salt and pepper, and serve.

MAKES: 4 SERVINGS

ROASTED CONFETTI RATATOUILLE

Confetti-like sparkles of tomato and warm-coloured peppers make this roasted take on ratatouille different from the average chunky, soupy mix. It's excellent as a base for grilled fish or even for a poached or fried egg.

1 orange pepper, finely diced
1 yellow pepper, finely diced
2 small zucchini, finely diced
2 small eggplants, finely diced
3 to 4 medium tomatoes, seeded and finely diced
3 garlic cloves, minced
1/4 cup (60 mL) olive oil, more as needed
Salt and pepper
A handful of sliced pitted black olives
A large handful of shredded fresh basil leaves

Heat the oven to 400°F (200°C). Toss together all the ingredients—except the olives and basil—and spread in a single layer on a large baking sheet (or 2 smaller baking sheets, depending on their size—you may need to work in batches). Bake, stirring once or twice, until tender, 20 to 25 minutes. Stir through the olives and basil and transfer to a serving dish. Serve warm or at room temperature.

MAKES: 6 TO 8 SERVINGS

DEEP-FRIED BROCCOLI
with HAZELNUT MAYONNAISE

. . . Or is this a first course? It's hard to choose. These feathery, crunchy, utterly addictive bites of broccoli can certainly be eaten on their own, but they also make a delicious side dish for grilled or baked fish. You're welcome to consider the hazelnut mayonnaise optional.

1 egg yolk

1 teaspoon Dijon mustard

1/2 teaspoon white wine vinegar

1/2 cup (125 mL) hazelnut oil

1/2 cup (125 mL) grapeseed oil

Salt and pepper

A squirt of lemon juice

A handful of hazelnuts, lightly toasted and chopped

1 pound (450 g) broccoli florets

Peanut or grapeseed oil, for frying

For the mayonnaise, in a small bowl, whisk together the yolk, mustard, and vinegar, then whisk in the hazelnut and grapeseed oils drop by drop until you have a smooth mayonnaise. Season with salt, pepper, and lemon juice. Stir in the hazelnuts. (The mayonnaise can be made several hours ahead. Cover and refrigerate.)

Break the broccoli florets into bite-sized pieces. Heat about 3 inches (8 cm) of the frying oil in a deep saucepan over medium heat. When sizzling (a rip of bread dropped in should immediately buzz and start turning golden), fry the broccoli, working in batches so as not to overcrowd, until golden. Remove to paper towels to drain and sprinkle with salt.

Serve the broccoli florets with the hazelnut mayonnaise for dipping.

MAKES: 6 SERVINGS

ROASTED CAULIFLOWER
with LENTILS *and* CAPERS

Roasting is one of the best methods for cooking cauliflower, a vegetable that, without a bit of colour, can border on boring. Here it's delicious, with the perkiness of capers, the crunch of toasted bread crumbs, and desirable earthiness from both the lentils and the walnut oil. You can use canned lentils, but I prefer to cook them myself because they're firmer and taste much better: put them in a pot with four times their volume of water, unsalted, along with a bay leaf, a thyme sprig, and a piece of onion. Simmer until al dente, about 25 minutes, then drain and rinse under cold water to stop the cooking.

1 head cauliflower, trimmed

3 tablespoons butter, melted

Salt and pepper

A few pinches of paprika

1 cup (200 g) cooked du Puy lentils, or more if you like

About 2 tablespoons walnut oil

1/2 cup (30 g) large fresh homemade bread crumbs (p. 207)

2 to 3 tablespoons capers

A generous handful of very finely chopped fresh parsley

Heat the oven to 400°F (200°C). Slice the cauliflower crosswise in about 1/2-inch (1 cm) slices (they will break apart somewhat) and arrange in a single layer on a baking sheet. Drizzle over the butter, season with salt and pepper, and sprinkle with paprika. Bake, turning occasionally, until tender and slightly golden, about 30 minutes.

Just before the cauliflower is done, gently warm the lentils for a minute or two with the walnut oil in a sauté pan. Season.

When the cauliflower is cooked, scatter the bread crumbs over top and return to the oven until they are toasted, 2 to 3 minutes. Mix with the lentils, capers, and parsley. Serve.

MAKES: 6 SERVINGS

How to Revive Frozen
or Day-Old Bread

I've never known a French person to do this, I must confess, but most of us are not French persons and fewer are living in France, so we must improvise. If you live within a stone's throw of a great Parisian bakery (which sometimes I do), read no further. If you live at the end of a logging road with not even reliable access to boat-delivered rusks (I've tried this, too), lend me your ears.

Frozen "French bread," once thawed, has an off-putting rubbery spring to it. This same bread can be revived so brilliantly that it will make you feel like you've just stepped out of an artisanal French bakery with a warm loaf tucked snugly under your arm. Of course, it's best if you thaw out what was a good loaf to begin with, but even inferior bread can be improved with this trick, and the trick is this:

First, thaw the bread in the microwave, which is a three-minute job. (I'm a microwave-free zone, myself, so my thawing takes longer: overnight on the counter.) Next, turn your regular oven on to 400°F (200°C), and when the oven is hot, place the loaf on the rack for 2 to 3 minutes until the crust is crisp. *Et voilà*: crusty crust with a warm soft crumb within. Pass the butter!

P.S. A Paris friend once taught me a trick for testing the quality of bread. You pinch off a piece, squish it in your fingers, and then set it on the palm of your hand. If it unfolds again to its original shape, it's good bread. ("See, it's alive!" exclaimed my friend.) If it stays squished . . . you need to find yourself a new baker.

FENNEL GRATIN

Few things are more French than this dish, nor as reassuringly, bubblingly comforting. The modern approach would be to replace the béchamel sauce below with an equivalent amount of crème fraîche, but I have to admit I find the old-fashioned version much better. As an alternative to bacon, you could wrap each piece of vegetable in a thin slice of ham. Leeks and endives work well here, too, halved lengthwise after boiling.

2 pounds (900 g) fennel (about 2 bulbs)
3 tablespoons butter
2 tablespoons flour
1-1/2 cups (375 mL) milk
Salt and pepper
4 slices bacon, cooked but not crisp, sliced
1/2 cup (30 g) fresh bread crumbs (p. 207)
1/2 cup (50 g) grated Gruyère or white Cheddar

Heat the oven to 375°F (190°C). Bring a large pot of salted water to a boil. Add the fennel and cook for 10 minutes. Drain, plunge into ice-cold water to stop the cooking, drain again, and dry well in a tea towel. Thickly slice the fennel lengthwise. Set aside.

For the béchamel sauce, melt the butter in a medium saucepan over medium heat. When the foaming has subsided, whisk in the flour and cook, whisking, for 1 minute. Whisk in the milk in a steady stream. Cook, stirring frequently, until thick, about 3 minutes. Remove from the heat and season with salt and pepper.

Arrange the fennel in a gratin dish, scattering over the bacon as you go. Pour over the sauce. Scatter over the bread crumbs and cheese. Bake until golden and bubbling, 15 to 20 minutes. Serve.

MAKES: 6 SERVINGS

GLAZED PEARL ONIONS *with* SAGE

We're coming close to candy with these rich, sweet, caramelized onions. You can't eat too many, but a few are an absolute treat alongside pork or even white fish. I'm told you can buy pearl onions already peeled, so if that step is a roadblock for you, feel free.

12 ounces (330 g) pearl onions
2 tablespoons butter
2 tablespoons sugar
1/4 cup (60 mL) water
Salt and pepper
A sprinkling of shredded fresh sage

Bring a pot of water to a boil and blanch the onions for 30 seconds. Drain and shock in ice-cold water. Drain again and peel.

Melt the butter in a sauté pan over medium heat and allow it to turn golden. Add the sugar, water, and onions. Season with salt and pepper. Cook, stirring often, until the onions are tender and coated in golden sauce, about 5 minutes.

Pour into a serving dish, scatter over the sage, and serve.

MAKES: 4 SERVINGS

BEET "GRATIN"

This gleaming ruby dish was the star at a dinner party not long ago, a magnificent accompaniment to pork. If you like the idea of a bit of crunch, butter-fried rye bread crumbs are delicious scattered over top. Just toast them in the oven at 350°F (180°C) for about 10 minutes until crisp.

4 medium beets (about 1-1/4 pounds/565 g), peeled
2 tablespoons olive oil
1 garlic clove, minced
Salt and pepper
A squirt of lemon juice
1 cup (250 mL) heavy cream
A handful of chopped fresh chervil or chives

Heat the oven to 375°F (190°C). Grate the beets on the large holes of a box grater. Heat the oil in a large frying pan, preferably cast iron, and sauté the beets with the garlic until soft, about 10 minutes. Season with salt, pepper, and lemon juice. Pour over the cream, and bake until the beets are tender and the cream is absorbed, about 20 minutes. Scatter over the chervil, and serve.

MAKES: 4 TO 6 SERVINGS

Les Restes

When the French say "*Tous les plats ne mérites pas êtres réchauffés*" ("Not all dishes are worth reheating"), it's relationships they're referring to, not yesterday's fricassée. I just throw that in, apropos of nothing, because I find the expression charming. Also I find it in contrast to the French practice with leftovers because I have rarely, rarely seen people throw food out. In fact, they take pride in being able to find the perfect use for even a leftover tablespoon of chopped-up mushrooms.

Some people seem afraid of leftovers, but to me they are one of the greatest joys of cooking. Take into consideration the fact that anything left over is generally already cooked, so that cuts time right from the get-go. Even better, leftovers are a fabulous way to increase your creative abilities in the kitchen. Sometimes they can even take you out of the kitchen. I'm assured by a neighbour that coffee grounds left over in the bottom of the breakfast pot are marvellous for exfoliating legs.

POTIRON PUMPKIN WEDGES
with ROSEMARY

If you're asked in France to bring home a "potiron," what you buy is a small, bright orange, teardrop-shaped pumpkin, nothing to do with giant pumpkins of the Hallowe'en variety. The potiron slices into nice melon-like wedges, making a dish that's bright and mellow-sweet at once, ideal for adding colour to the table when a main dish seems, however tasty, a bit banal in its brownness. Butternut squash is a good alternative if, searching high and low outside France, you don't come across a potiron.

1 potiron or butternut squash (about 1-1/2 pounds/675 g)
About 2 tablespoons butter
Salt and pepper
A drizzling of olive oil
A handful of chopped fresh rosemary

Heat the oven to 400°F (200°C). Halve the pumpkin lengthwise and seed it, then cut into wedges like a melon. Rub the flesh of each wedge with butter and season with salt and pepper. Lay on a baking sheet. Drizzle with olive oil, scatter over the rosemary, and bake until soft, about an hour. Serve.

MAKES: 4 SERVINGS

TURNIPS *in* MISO BUTTER

Few vegetables turn out tastier than these turnips, lovely as a second side dish alongside steamed greens of any sort. Japan meets France . . . and if this recipe is any indication, the two should meet more often.

1 pound (450 g) small white turnips
2 tablespoons butter
1 tablespoon red or white miso paste, more to taste
1/2 cup (125 mL) water
Freshly ground pepper

Peel and quarter the turnips. Melt the butter in a large sauté pan, add the miso, and whisk in the water. Stir in the turnips. Cover and simmer until approaching tender, 10 to 15 minutes. Uncover and continue cooking, stirring occasionally, until the juices have reduced around the vegetable to a thin sauce, about 5 minutes longer. Season with pepper, and serve.

MAKES: 4 SERVINGS

COCOTTE *of* WINTER VEGETABLES *with* CRÈME FRAÎCHE

This pretty and comforting stew of winter vegetables can accompany roast pork, pot roast of beef, or even just a few fried sausages. I decided against parsnips here, but depending on what meat you're serving, you may want to consider them sometime when you're in the mood for extra sweetness.

1 tablespoon butter

2 slices bacon, thinly sliced

1 bay leaf

1/2 cup (125 mL) chicken stock, more if needed

6 wedges (2 inches/5 cm) green cabbage

3 small turnips, peeled and cut into 8 wedges each

2 carrots, peeled and cut into batons

1/2 small rutabaga, peeled and sliced 1/4 inch (5 mm) thick

Salt and pepper

1/2 cup (125 mL) crème fraîche

A handful of chopped fresh parsley, tarragon, or chervil

Melt the butter in a flameproof casserole or Dutch oven. Add the bacon and gently cook, without allowing it to crispen, 3 to 5 minutes. Toss in the bay leaf, pour in the stock, add the vegetables, and season with salt and pepper. Cover and simmer, without stirring, until the vegetables are tender, about 20 minutes, checking towards the end to make sure the pan has not gone dry. Add a bit more stock if it has.

Add the crème fraîche and stir to blend into the sauce. Tumble into a serving dish, scatter over the chopped herb, add perhaps an additional grinding of pepper, and serve.

MAKES: 6 SERVINGS

APPLE *and* RED ONION COMPOTE

This may be the single most beautiful and feminine dish I've ever seen in my life. From cooking, the skins of green apples go yellow, the red go pink, and the plum-hued onion threads itself among them. The friend who gave this recipe to me makes it with foie gras in the middle: a whole deveined lobe simply sandwiched between the apple and onion and which, once cooked, gets sliced and served alongside as a first course. Even without that special treatment, this side dish elevates many a dinner, say a creamy chicken sauté, pork roast, or confit duck legs. Stunning.

2 Royal Gala apples

2 Granny Smith apples

1 medium red onion, sliced

A handful of fresh thyme leaves

1/4 cup (55 g) butter, cut into small dice

Salt and pepper

1 teaspoon cider vinegar

Cut each apple into 8 wedges and remove the core. Put a layer of apples in a medium saucepan, followed by a layer of onion, thyme, and butter. Season with salt and pepper. Continue layering until all the ingredients have been used up. Sprinkle over the vinegar. Cover and cook over low heat, without stirring, until the apples and onions are just tender, about 15 minutes. Serve.

MAKES: 4 TO 6 SERVINGS

FONDANT GARLIC BUTTER POTATOES

Here, garlic butter infuses the potatoes right to the core. If you put these on the table, they will disappear. Guaranteed.

1-1/2 pounds (675 g) small red and white potatoes
1/4 cup (55 g) butter
4 garlic cloves, crushed
Salt and pepper
A handful of chopped fresh chives or parsley

Put everything—except the chives—in a large saucepan and heat to melt the butter. Cover and cook over very low heat, shaking the pan occasionally, until the potatoes are meltingly tender, about 20 minutes, depending on the size of the potatoes. Toss with the chives, and serve.

MAKES: 4 SERVINGS

CRUSHED NEW POTATOES *with* BLACK OLIVES *and* CHERRY TOMATOES

A simple enough idea, but somehow it delivers even more than it promises. This is a wonderfully casual side dish for summer.

1 pound (450 g) small new potatoes
2 tablespoons butter
1 tablespoon olive oil
Salt and pepper
8 to 10 cherry tomatoes, quartered
8 to 10 black olives, pitted and chopped
A handful of chopped fresh chives or parsley

Bring a pot of water to a boil. Salt it and add the potatoes. Gently boil until tender, about 20 minutes. Drain. Add the butter and oil, then season with salt and pepper. Crush the potatoes slightly using the back of a wooden spoon. Stir through the tomatoes and olives. Scatter over the chives, and serve.

MAKES: 4 SERVINGS

New Life for White Plates

I remember the first time I saw a set of all-white dinnerware. It was in the eighties and I thought it was the chicest stuff I'd ever seen, stacked as it was against the dark wooden shelves of a friend's mother's kitchen. Then, apparently, the whole world decided white china looked chic and suddenly it was nearly impossible to buy anything else. But all-white dishes do seem a bit clinical after a while, and a little imagination applied to them occasionally can be a great relief.

Antique floral side plates and bowls to mix and match with the white, for instance, give the table an instant bohemian feel and make me feel like I live in a chic little apartment in Montmartre. They're cheap at flea markets and I'm forever on the lookout. Another way to make white dishes look sophisticated but without the ice-queen factor is to lay them on good-quality off-white, cream, and/or grey linens. Somehow layering white and other like-minded hues lends warmth to the table, even though they're coolish shades themselves. This is very French.

For anyone really artistic, the solution is to go colour crazy everywhere under-neath and around those loo-white dishes. My friend Ivan is genius at this. He has loads of coloured glasses and tablecloths that he mixes and matches and layers to high heaven to create a look that's modern but not remotely minimalist. If you can imagine such a thing as "streamlined maximalism," I'd say that's his sig-nature look. Watching him work his magic with a table is just the kind of inspi-ration to convince me that I perhaps shouldn't toss my stash of white porcelain china quite yet after all.

SCHOOL NIGHT POTATO PURÉE

A French mother's way of sneaking a few more vegetables into her children's diet, this cheerful purée (one friend calls it "happy mash") is smooth, comforting, and delicious.

2 pounds (900 g) floury potatoes, peeled and cut into chunks
1 celery rib, peeled and thinly sliced
1 carrot, peeled and grated
1/4 cup (55 g) butter
1/4 cup (60 mL) milk, preferably warm
Salt and pepper

Bring a pot of water to a boil. Salt it and add the vegetables. Simmer until everything is tender, about 20 minutes. Drain and mash with the butter and milk. Season and serve.

MAKES: 4 TO 6 SERVINGS

DUCK FAT POTATOES

It is amazing what a big difference simply changing the fat can make to a recipe. Duck fat makes potatoes ultra-crisp, and the flavour is out of this world.

1 pound (450 g) Yukon Gold potatoes
2 to 3 tablespoons duck fat, melted
Salt and pepper
A handful of chopped fresh parsley

Heat the oven to 375°F (190°C). Scrub the potatoes or, if they're not organic, peel them. Cut into long wedges. Toss with the fat and season with salt and pepper. Spread in a single layer on a baking sheet and bake, stirring once or twice, until golden and crisp, 30 to 40 minutes. Scatter over the parsley and tilt into a serving dish. Serve.

MAKES: 4 SERVINGS

TWO-POTATO GRATIN

This attractive gratin, made with stock instead of cream, positively melts in the mouth. The cheese lends creaminess, richness, and flavour, but you hardly know it's there.

6 tablespoons (90 g) butter
1 sweet potato (about 1 pound/450 g), peeled and thinly sliced crosswise
1-1/2 pounds (675 g) waxy potatoes such as Yukon Gold (about 4 medium),
    peeled and thinly sliced crosswise
Salt and pepper
1 onion, chopped
1 to 2 garlic cloves, minced (optional)
A few handfuls of finely chopped fresh parsley and/or thyme
4 ounces (110 g) Comté, Gruyère, or white Cheddar, grated (about 1 cup/250 mL)
A handful of finely grated Parmesan cheese
1-1/2 cups (375 mL) rich homemade beef or chicken stock

Heat the oven to 400°F (200°C). Smear 2 tablespoons of the butter over the bottom of an 8-cup (2 L) gratin dish, then melt the rest.

Lay a quarter of the potato slices, overlapping slightly, in the dish. Season with salt and pepper, sprinkle over a third of the butter, and scatter over a third of the onion, garlic (if using), and parsley. Sprinkle over half of the Gruyère. Repeat layering in the same manner, finishing with a layer of potatoes. Season and sprinkle with a little more parsley. Sprinkle over the Parmesan cheese.

Bring the stock to a boil and pour into one corner of the baking dish. It will distribute itself without washing away your careful layering. Bake until the potatoes are very tender and melded together, the stock having been completely absorbed, about an hour and 15 minutes. Serve hot.

MAKES: 6 TO 8 SERVINGS

Ode to Bread Crumbs

A kitchen without homemade bread crumbs is like a cold day and no hat. You must have bread crumbs in the house, and at least two kinds. The bread crumbs I use most often, I make on the spur of the moment, with either fresh or day-old bread. Simply put the bread, baguette, or whatever you've got, pulled into large chunks, into a food processor and pulse to the size of panko flakes. These are the crumbs you need for topping gratins, toasting in butter to strew over soups or salads, rolling fish cakes in, making stuffings...and on and on it goes. They freeze well, too.

Fine dried bread crumbs, the kind as fine as sand, are another matter. For these, you must use dry bread chunks and whiz them in the processor until they are reduced practically to dust. Then you put them through a sifter. These fine crumbs are useful for replacing flour in certain cakes and for dusting buttered pans to prevent sticking. They are also useful for breading anything you plan to fry with a very light coating; the crumbs will create a slightly crunchy and very fetching golden exterior.

EGG NOODLES
with GREEN PEPPERCORNS

Green peppercorns have a woodsy, almost pine-like taste that is delicious against pasta. This dish is wonderful with braised meats, especially game, or ragouts, but I'm perfectly capable of eating a bowlful all on its own. For a richer taste, should the occasion demand it, brown the butter before adding.

8 ounces (225 g) pappardelle or wide egg noodles
2 tablespoons butter, melted
2 tablespoons drained green peppercorns in brine, lightly crushed

Bring a pot of water to a boil. Salt it, add the pappardelle, and cook until al dente. Drain and toss with the butter and peppercorns. Serve.

MAKES: 4 TO 6 SERVINGS

COUSCOUS *with* CURRANTS

An easy-to-eat side dish to serve with Chicken and Orange Tagine (p. 122) or with Fork and Spoon Lamb (p. 141).

2 tablespoons butter
1/2 onion, minced
2 cups (375 g) medium-grain couscous
1-1/2 cups (375 mL) chicken stock
1 cup (250 mL) water
1/4 cup (40 g) currants
Salt and pepper

Melt the butter in a saucepan and gently fry the onion until soft, about 5 minutes. Stir in the couscous, stock, water, and currants. Season with salt and pepper. Bring to a boil, cover, and turn off the heat. Wait 15 minutes, or until the liquid is completely absorbed. Fluff with a fork and transfer to a serving dish.

MAKES: 8 SERVINGS

BURNT ANGEL HAIR
with GREEN ONIONS

I learned to make this unusual dish in the French countryside, and it was such a neat trick the recipe followed me back to Paris. It's beefy flavoured, fine textured, and, above all, fun to make. I like it as a base for grilled seafood or fish.

2 tablespoons butter
8 ounces (225 g) angel hair pasta, broken in pieces
2 envelopes or cubes beef bouillon powder
2 green onions, thinly sliced

Bring about 2 cups (500 mL) water to a boil. Meanwhile, melt the butter in a sauté pan over medium-high heat. When it's foaming, add the pasta and toast, stirring, until the pasta turns a deep golden colour, about 5 minutes. Sprinkle over the stock powder and pour over just enough boiling water to cover. Slap on a lid and leave over low heat until the water is completely absorbed, about 5 minutes longer. Scatter over the green onions, and serve.

MAKES: 4 SERVINGS

RIZ *au* LIT

One nutty Parisian neighbour of mine—an art restorer, as it happened—had no end of tricks up her sleeve for dealing with household troubles. This was her way of making rice ahead of time and keeping it warm. You wrap it up and put it in your bed. Obviously.

1 cup (200 g) basmati rice
1 tablespoon butter
4 cups (1 L) stock or water (or half of each)
Salt and pepper

Rinse the rice in cold water and drain. Melt the butter in a medium pot, stir in the rice, then pour in the stock. Season with salt and pepper. Cover and simmer (do not boil) until tender, 7 to 8 minutes.

Keeping the lid on, remove from the heat, wrap the pot in a bath towel, and stick it under a pillow until ready to serve—ideally within an hour or two.

MAKES: 4 SERVINGS

BEER *and* BUCKWHEAT CRÊPES

The addition of brew to crêpes gives them an irresistible ghostly yeasty depth, which, paired with a hint of buckwheat, raises them far above the average bland, white variety. I like to set these on the table as a side dish, flat or folded into triangles (they're great for mopping up sauce from, say, a creamy chicken sauté). My other favourite trick is to brush crêpes with butter, cut them into strips, and toast until crisp in a 375°F (190°C) oven; these make excellent crackers for soup. And an idea I've yet to try but am most intrigued by is that of sandwiching these with grated cheese and frying them like quesadillas to be cut into wedges. For those more conventionally inclined, use them to upgrade leftover chicken, ham, spinach, or mushrooms: simply stir your leftovers into a béchamel sauce (p. 186), roll them in the crêpes, set them in a baking dish, scatter over grated cheese, and bake in a hot oven until bubbling and golden.

2 eggs
3/4 cup (95 g) flour
1/2 cup (60 g) light buckwheat flour
1-1/4 cups (300 mL) milk
1 cup (250 mL) dark beer, such as Guinness
6 tablespoons (90 g) salted butter, melted
Salt and pepper (optional)

Lightly whisk the eggs in a medium bowl, then add the remaining ingredients, seasoning if you like, and whisk until the batter is smooth. Transfer to a jug and let sit at room temperature for 2 hours.

Heat a 6-inch (15 cm) crêpe pan or frying pan, which you've rubbed with oil, over medium-low heat. Stir the batter well. Lift the pan off the burner and pour in about a tablespoon of batter, tilting the pan in all directions as you do so to cover the bottom of the pan. Cook until the underside is starting to turn golden, about 2 minutes, then flip and finish, about 30 seconds more. Repeat, stirring the batter before pouring each crêpe. As the crêpes come off the pan, stack them on a plate and keep them warm in a low oven.

MAKES: ABOUT 28 (6-INCH/15 CM) CRÊPES

POLENTA *with* BLUE CHEESE *en* TERRINE

Yes, polenta is Italian, but in my friend Camille's hands, it gets the Parisian touch with crème fraîche, blue cheese, and thyme. Creamy, tangy, perfect with pork, and, once it's in the terrine, the kind of thing that can be made ahead and gently reheated before serving.

1 cup (250 mL) water
1 cup (250 mL) milk
1 cup (125 g) instant polenta
1/3 cup (75 mL) crème fraîche
A handful of chopped fresh thyme
2 tablespoons grated Parmesan cheese
Salt and pepper
3 ounces (85 g) creamy blue cheese, crumbled or in pinches

Bring the water and milk to a boil in a medium saucepan. Salt it. Add the polenta in a thin stream, whisking as you go. Cook, stirring, to the texture of porridge. Stir in the crème fraîche, thyme, and Parmesan cheese. Season lightly with salt and generously with pepper.

Spoon half the polenta mixture into a 4-cup (1 L) terrine, spreading it evenly with a spatula if needed. Sprinkle evenly with the blue cheese, then spoon the remainder of the mixture on top. (If not baking right away, cool completely, cover, and refrigerate.)

Twenty minutes before serving, heat the oven to 350°F (180°C). Put the lid on the terrine and put in the oven to heat through, 15 to 20 minutes. Serve from the terrine.

MAKES: 4 TO 6 SERVINGS

DESS

ERTS

DESSERTS

GRAPEFRUIT *in* CARAMEL

This is my kind of dessert: a gorgeous and glistening pink and amber jewel pool that juxtaposes slightly bitter caramel and acidic citrus. It's refreshing and interesting, perfect to end a serious feast, which may explain why I've been known to trot this out on New Year's Eve.

6 pink grapefruit
1 cup (200 g) sugar

Cut the top and bottom from each grapefruit using a sharp knife, then, working top to bottom, cut off all the skin and white pith from the fruit. Holding each fruit over a bowl, cut between the membranes to release the sections, letting them fall into the bowl. Remove the pips as you find them. Squeeze the membranes over the bowl to extract any further juice. Strain the juice into a cup and drink it.

Melt the sugar in a large skillet with 2 tablespoons water over medium-high heat, stirring to dissolve. When the liquid is clear, stop stirring, and boil until the mixture reaches a dark caramel, about 5 minutes. Drizzle over the grapefruit. (The caramel will seize, but don't worry, it will melt as it sits.) Cover and refrigerate for at least an hour, until the caramel has completely melted around the fruit. Serve cold.

MAKES: 6 SERVINGS

Private Label

A great delight of mine in Paris is the glorious packaging on luxury foods: oh, the pretty sugars and jars of oil, the crocks of mustards and boxes of chocolates…It's a feast for the eyes better than any jewellery shop! Even some otherwise pedestrian grocery-store goods reach these heights. The creamy vanilla yogurt that comes in terracotta pots painted forget-me-not blue comes to mind…

I may be alone in this, although I doubt it, but the sight of ugly packaging depresses me no end. (I'm still furious at Arm & Hammer for retiring the pretty pastoral Cow Brand baking soda box.) It's not always I can keep up with this, but to an extent I try: part of my grocery unpacking ritual is to repackage anything that offends my eyes. Dried fruits and nuts that come in plastic, for example, are unattractive to begin with, and once opened they're also messy, so into jars they go post-haste. Ditto legumes and grains of any sort, even flour and sugar, which belong in their trusty bins. As you may have noticed, many commercial packagers of herbs and spices have never heard of the teaspoon, which I suppose is their excuse for packaging their offerings in little bottles with openings no bigger than a peephole. A friend of mine was posted for work in Nepal for a few years, and she once arrived in Paris to visit with about 50 metal spice canisters as a gift. I was out of my wits with excitement! I made my own labels, written with a fountain pen, emptied all my spices into them, and lined them up in a single row on a looooong shelf where I could gloat over them at leisure. In one of my multitudinous moves, those tins were lost. I've been in the market for a new brigade ever since.

SOUFFLÉD APPLES
with SUGARED RYE CRUMBS

These apples puff up magically like airy soufflés, making a very nice family dessert. The rye crumbs are optional, but do give lovely crunch. To make them, whiz 2 ounces (55 g) dark rye bread in the food processor to coarse crumbs. This will result in about a cup. Scatter them on a baking sheet with 2 tablespoons of brown sugar, toss, and crisp them in a 325°F (160°C) oven until golden, about 10 minutes. (These can also be done in a frying pan on the stovetop while the apples bake, but it's slightly trickier to get even browning.) Toasted slivered almonds are another option. Scatter either over the apples just before serving.

4 to 6 baking apples
4 to 6 teaspoons butter
4 to 6 teaspoons white or brown sugar
A scant sprinkling of cinnamon or nutmeg
Sugared rye bread crumbs, for serving (see headnote; optional)

Heat the oven to 400°F (200°C).

Peel the apples and halve lengthwise, leaving the stem on where possible. Core the apples, using a melon baller or small spoon, and set in a baking dish core side up. Put 1/2 teaspoon of butter in each cavity, and sprinkle over the sugar and cinnamon. Bake until puffed up, soft all the way through, and golden on top from the sugar, about 40 minutes, depending on the size of the apples.

Scatter over the crunchy bread crumbs (if using) and serve with vanilla ice cream.

MAKES: 4 TO 6 SERVINGS

RETRO PINEAPPLE

Perhaps this sounds like a joke, but wait until you set it in front of your guests! It's an instant memory maker, I promise, an impressive finale for when you want a light end to dinner that takes no effort.

1 large pineapple
A few tablespoons of orange juice or a splash of rum or orange liqueur

Using a large knife, cut the pineapple, including the leaves, in half lengthwise. Using a sharp paring knife, carefully cut the flesh out of each half, leaving the skins intact. Cut out and discard the tough core. Cut the flesh into cubes. Toss with the juice in a bowl, then cover and refrigerate for at least an hour. Put the skins in a plastic bag and refrigerate.

Divide the marinated cubes between the 2 pineapple skins on a platter, and serve.

MAKES: 6 SERVINGS

BAKED PEARS *with* BLUEBERRIES

A pear baked with butter, vanilla sugar, and a scraping of nutmeg is beautiful in its own right, but if you're looking for something more colourful and original, this is your ticket. The pears emerge their soft, fragrant selves with blueberries slumped all around them into a brilliant purple sauce.

4 pears, peeled, halved, and cored
1/2 cup (75 g) wild low-bush blueberries
6 tablespoons sugar
4 teaspoons butter
A drizzle of cassis or blueberry liqueur (optional)

Heat the oven to 400°F (200°C). Lay the pear halves in a baking dish just large enough to hold them. Scatter over the blueberries, followed by the sugar. Put 1/2 teaspoon of butter on each pear half. Drizzle over a judicious amount of liqueur, if using.

Cover with foil and bake until the pears are perfectly tender, about 45 minutes. Serve the pear halves with the blueberry juices spooned over.

MAKES: 4 TO 8 SERVINGS

POACHED GREEN FIGS

Boring name, divine dish. It is utter ease to make, but make sure you have some time because, although you're not actually doing any work, the figs need to simmer a long time. It's well worth the wait, believe me: the bright green figs you started with will turn a glistening candied chartreuse as they cool in the figgy-flavoured syrup. One per person is enough, because they're quite rich.

2 cups (390 g) sugar
1 cup (250 mL) water
8 firm but ripe green figs (about 2-1/2 ounces/70 g each)
1 lemon wedge

Put the sugar in a saucepan wide enough to accommodate the figs in a single layer. Pour over the water and heat to dissolve the sugar. When the sugar has dissolved, add the figs. Bring to a boil, then reduce heat to a gentle simmer for 1 hour.

Remove the figs with a slotted spoon to a serving dish. Bring the syrup to a vigorous boil and reduce to sauce consistency, about 20 minutes. You'll know it's close to sauce consistency when the surface bubbles become very big, as in a bubble bath, so watch closely then. Pour the syrup over the figs and cool. Serve with custard sauce, or with fresh cheese, or with cream you've whipped with about one-quarter mascarpone.

MAKES: 8 SERVINGS

BROILED BANANAS
on the HALF SHELL

Have faith! I know this sounds underwhelming, but broiled bananas, ridiculously simple though they are, are absolutely delicious. And they're fun, too; I love spooning the soft, caramelized flesh right from the peel. A scoop of vanilla ice cream and a crisp cookie on each plate complete the dish. (Try the cookies on pp. 273 and 277.) You might like to pass the rum bottle, too, if you have devils in your midst.

3 bananas
6 to 8 teaspoons sugar

Heat the broiler with the rack near the top. Cut the bananas in half lengthwise and lay them cut side up on a baking sheet. Sprinkle sugar over the flesh. Broil until caramelized on top, about 5 minutes.

Put a banana half on each plate with a ball of vanilla ice cream alongside. Serve at once.

MAKES: 6 SERVINGS

A Way to Serve Stone Fruits or Strawberries in Summer

One of the most enchanting ideas I have ever seen is this one for serving stone fruits and fragile things like strawberries. If you pre-wash these fruits, which are delicate, and have them sitting and waiting and waiting in a serving bowl, they tend to get mooshy. The solution, and one that adds romance to dinner like crazy, is not to wash the fruit but instead to serve it in one bowl along with *another* bowl, preferably crystal or cut glass, which you've filled with cold water and ice cubes. The idea (and of course at this point you're sitting on a terrace after a lazy and rather boozy late-summer lunch) is that people select their pieces of fruit from the first bowl and then dip them into the ice water bowl to clean them before raising them to their lips. Imagine: sweet, sun-ripened fruit, juicy-warm inside and fresh outside... like your very own self, after a leisurely jog, say, followed by a dip in a lake.

It's all rather raccoony in a way, which doesn't sound overly Parisian, but you see, with a crystal bowl of ice water we've made it chic, and it is wonderfully participatory to dip fruit this way and then eat it, juice running from your lips. It slows the whole meal down, in a pastoral way, and even if you have a view of the wretched Montparnasse, it makes you feel like you could be in the *fin fond de nulle part*, perhaps on a stone August terrace in Provence or on holiday *parmi les vignes* not far from Bergerac...

STRAWBERRIES *and* CREAMS

There is no point eating a strawberry unless it's in season, ripe, and red the whole way through. On the rare occasions when one does happen upon such a delicacy, there's no better way to eat them than as simply as possible, which is the territory we're treading here.

1 pound (450 g) fresh, ripe strawberries
2 tablespoons sugar, to taste
1/2 cup (125 mL) crème fraîche
1/2 cup (125 mL) heavy cream
2 tablespoons orange liqueur, amaretto, kirsch, or whisky

Trim the strawberries and cut in half. Toss with the sugar, cover, and refrigerate for 1 hour. Whip the creams together with the alcohol to soft peaks. Cover and refrigerate.

Bring the berries to room temperature before serving. Spoon them into serving dishes, top with a dollop of cream, and dribble over the berry juices.

MAKES: 6 SERVINGS

RHUBARB FOOL

A pretty, billowing, marbled springtime dessert that's utterly fuss-free and impossible not to love. I think it's perfect as is, but should you find yourself with gorgeous ripe strawberries at hand, don't hesitate to serve them alongside. You can also garnish it with broken-up meringue, even stirred through if you like, although if you're taking that route you may want to omit the sugar in the whipped cream.

2 pounds (900 g) chopped fresh or frozen rhubarb
1-1/4 cups (255 g) sugar
1-1/2 cups (375 mL) heavy cream
A few drops of vanilla

Put the rhubarb in a pot with 1 cup (200 g) of the sugar. Bring to a simmer and stew, stirring occasionally, until the rhubarb turns to soft threads, about 10 minutes. (If you've used frozen rhubarb, you may have to simmer it longer to cook off any excess water.) Cool to room temperature.

Whip the cream with 1/4 cup (55 g) sugar and the vanilla to soft peaks. Stir through the rhubarb for a marbled effect and spill into an attractive serving bowl. Cover and chill for a few hours before serving.

MAKES: 8 SERVINGS

COFFEE ICE BRICK

I am not a fan of bought ice creams generally, but neither am I keen on messing about with ice-cream makers, if I can avoid it. Besides, what Parisian kitchen has room for one? If coffee is not your bag of tricks, stir through some crushed fresh berries or chopped peaches instead.

2 cups (500 mL) heavy cream
2/3 cup (150 mL) sweetened condensed milk
1 tablespoon instant espresso powder
1/4 teaspoon vanilla

Line a loaf pan with plastic wrap. Put everything in a large bowl and beat with an electric mixer until the mixture is the consistency of thick whipped cream. Pour into the loaf pan, cover, and freeze.

Remove from the freezer a few minutes before serving. Dip the base and sides of the loaf pan into warm water for a few seconds to loosen, then turn the ice out onto a chilled platter. Remove the plastic wrap and slice to serve.

MAKES: 6 TO 8 SERVINGS

𝒜 BLACKBERRY SORBET . . . *of sorts*

This isn't a true sorbet. It cuts a corner by not using sugar syrup, and results in a vaguely granita-textured affair bursting with blackberry flavour. As a bonus, the bothersome seeds are eliminated, so there's nothing to interfere with the enjoyment of the taste. A scoop served with an equal-sized scoop of vanilla ice cream alongside is magic making.

2 pounds (900 g) fresh or frozen blackberries
3/4 to 1 cup (155 to 200 g) sugar, depending on sweetness of berries
A squeeze of lemon juice
2 egg whites

Stir together the berries, sugar, and lemon juice. Let sit for 10 minutes to help dissolve the sugar, then purée with an immersion blender. Press through a fine-mesh sieve using a ladle (best tool for the job); discard the seeds. Pour the liquid into a cake pan and freeze just until slushy—not crystallized or in shards—about 2 hours. (This depends on your freezer, so check every half-hour the first time you make this.)

Whisk the egg whites to soft peaks and fold into the berry mixture. Refreeze until solid, a few hours. Serve with vanilla ice cream.

MAKES: 8 SERVINGS

CRÈME FRAÎCHE ICE CREAM

I avoid ice-cream makers when I can, but here you can't. Besides, this ice cream is so heavenly, I'd be prepared to haul out a cement mixer to make it if I had to. If you can't find crème fraîche, Greek yogurt also works, making a cleaner, slightly more sorbet-like variation of this tangy, creamy ice.

2 cups (500 mL) crème fraîche
3/4 cup (155 g) sugar
1/2 cup (125 mL) heavy cream
Zest and juice of 1 lemon

Stir all the ingredients together, then freeze in an ice-cream churner according to the manufacturer's instructions. Serve.

MAKES: 8 SERVINGS

FROZEN GRAND MARNIER SOUFFLÉ

Here is a light and fluffy finish to follow a meaty, wintery dinner. Serve cookies on the side for a crumbly contrast.

4 egg whites
1 cup (200 g) sugar
1 cup (250 mL) heavy cream
1/4 cup (60 mL) Grand Marnier
2 oranges

Whisk the whites to stiff peaks. Whisk in the sugar, a spoonful at a time, to make a stiff, glossy meringue. In another bowl, whip the cream, adding the Grand Marnier at the end. Zest the oranges and scatter the zest over the whites, reserving the oranges. Fold the cream and whites together. Transfer to a serving dish, cover, and freeze until firm, several hours or overnight.

Remove the pith from the oranges with a sharp knife. Cut between the membranes to remove the sections and transfer to a bowl. Before serving the soufflé, drain the juice from the orange sections (reserve for another use) and use the orange for decoration.

MAKES: 8 SERVINGS

Add Dash to Your Dollops

This may sound obvious, because it's such a simple notion, but it's the kind of thing that can slip your mind, and when you're reminded of it again it's eye-widening in the most pleasurable of ways. Whipped cream, especially when it's ever-so-slightly sweetened with sugar and further enhanced with a drop or two of vanilla, is a topping that goes with almost anything and which everybody seems to like. The French call it *crème Chantilly*.

Wonderful stuff, but there can be so much more to whipped cream than that. Obviously, you can use brown sugar in place of white, or use even maple syrup or honey to vary flavour. You can also skip vanilla and pry open the booze cupboard. Whisky whipped cream, I'm sure I don't have to tell you, knocks socks off when spooned alongside poached pears. Then, depending on whether you're spooning onto fruit, cake, or pudding, the choices are endless: Cognac, rum, orange liqueur, amaretto, kirsch, rose water, orange flower water … let your imagination run wild. Also, whipped cream has a place in savoury cooking. Stir a spoonful of it into lemony mayonnaise for an instant sauce for cold fish. Fold it into horseradish sauce for a little topping for cold roast beef. And if you really want to raise eyebrows, put a dollop on top of bowls of hot soup and blast for a few seconds under the broiler until the cream browns just slightly.

COFFEE JELLY

When I first tried this, it was on a whim, because, frankly, it didn't sound very nice. Well, like some of those people you meet on the path of life whom you think you're not going to like, but who, in the end, turn out to be your best friends, this has become one of my favourite desserts. It's very grown-up: slightly bitter, cold and refreshing, exquisitely light, and jelled to wobbly perfection. Make this in the morning while the coffee pot is full of hot brew, then dessert will be all set when you arrive home in the evening. If you're going to be serving this at a late hour, you may want to use decaffeinated coffee. Whatever the case, make sure the coffee is not too strong or the dessert will be bitter.

1/2 cup (125 mL) cold coffee (medium strength)
1 envelope powdered gelatin (1 tablespoon)
1-1/4 cups (300 mL) hot medium-strength black Americano coffee
Whipped cream and dark chocolate, for serving
(No, there is no sugar in this dessert.)

Put the cold coffee in a medium heatproof bowl and sprinkle over the gelatin. Set aside to soften for a minute. Set the bowl over a pan of barely simmering water and stir for a minute to dissolve the gelatin thoroughly; the mixture should be clear. Remove the bowl from the pan.

Stir the hot coffee into the gelatin mixture. The gelatin should be completely dissolved and the mixture should look like regular coffee. Divide evenly among 4 serving glasses. Cool, cover, and refrigerate until set, 3 to 4 hours.

To serve, top with slightly sweetened whipped cream (flavoured with alcohol or not), and grate over dark chocolate.

MAKES: 4 SERVINGS

POSSET *for* PARISIANS

I'm not going to pretend this is a French recipe because it's as English as Shakespeare and has been around at least that long, albeit in varied forms. I think it was originally a drink made of wine and milk boiled together, which I hope didn't taste as vile as it sounds. Now, mercifully, it's a cold pudding very similar to a lemon pot de crème, only, magically, without any egg! Everyone loves it (im*posset*ible not to love posset!), especially an overstretched cook because it takes a grand total of three minutes to make.

1-1/2 cups (375 mL) heavy cream
1/2 cup (125 mL) sugar
Zest of 1 lemon
1/2 cup (125 mL) lemon juice

Put all the ingredients in a saucepan much larger than you think you need. Bring it to a boil (if you have a big enough pot, it won't boil over) and boil for 2 minutes. Pour into demitasse cups or small glasses and set aside to cool. Cover and refrigerate for an hour or so until custard-firm. Serve straight from the refrigerator.

MAKES: 6 TO 8 SERVINGS

SALTED CARAMEL POTS *de* CRÈME

A very, very dangerous dessert worth saving room for, but be warned: it has created more than one addict.

1 cup (200 g) sugar
1-1/2 cups (375 mL) heavy cream
1/2 cup (125 mL) whole milk
6 egg yolks
Fleur de sel

Heat the oven to 325°F (160°C). Bring a large kettle of water to a boil. Set six 1/2-cup (125 mL) ramekins in a shallow baking pan.

Melt the sugar in a skillet with 1/4 cup (60 mL) water over medium-high heat, stirring until the sugar has dissolved. Stop stirring and cook to amber caramel, about 8 minutes. Standing well back (the mixture will sputter), whisk in the cream and milk. Whisk the yolks in a medium bowl, then slowly stir in the milk mixture. Strain into a jug or large measuring cup.

Pour the custard into the ramekins. Set the baking dish in the oven, then pour in hot water from the kettle to come halfway up the sides of the ramekins. Cover the dish with foil. Bake until the custard has just the slightest, slightest sense of wobble in the centre, about 30 minutes.

Remove the ramekins from the water bath and cool completely on a rack. Cover and chill until serving. Serve with a pinch of fleur de sel atop each.

MAKES: 6 SERVINGS

MOCHA CHOCOLATE MOUSSE *MINUTE*

Fast, fabulous, and, as it happens, fat- and dairy-free, although I, of course, pile on whipped cream to serve, which completely negates that bit of boasting.

4 ounces (110 g) 70% chocolate

1/4 cup (60 mL) hot espresso

4 eggs, separated

1 tablespoon Cognac, rum, kirsch, or orange liqueur

In a small heatproof bowl set over a pot of barely simmering water, gently melt the chocolate with the coffee, stirring until smooth. Remove from the pot and set aside.

In a medium bowl, beat the egg yolks with the liqueur, then stir in the chocolate in a thin stream. The mixture will be thick.

In another bowl, beat the egg whites to stiff peaks. Stir a generous spoonful into the chocolate mixture to loosen it, then pour the chocolate mixture over the remaining whites and gently fold to combine.

Transfer to a serving dish or dishes, cover, and refrigerate for at least 2 hours before serving.

MAKES: 4 SERVINGS

CRACKED DARK CHOCOLATE PUDDING

I was served this for my birthday once and it was instant love for what is a sort of cross between a mousse and a cake, boasting an airy, intensely chocolaty base with a cracked, crunchy meringue-like top. You'll want to buy excellent chocolate for this dessert, because chocolate is indeed what you taste. Feel free to splash in some rum or espresso for flavouring if you like.

3/4 cup + 2 tablespoons (200 g) butter, cut into pieces
7 ounces (200 g) high-quality dark chocolate, chopped
4 eggs, separated
3/4 to 1 cup (155 to 200 g) sugar, to taste

Heat the oven to 400°F (200°C). Lightly grease an 8-inch (20 cm) square baking dish.

In a heatproof bowl set over a pot of barely simmering water, gently melt the butter and chocolate together, stirring until smooth. Remove from the pot and set aside.

In a medium bowl, beat the egg whites until they just hold peaks, then beat in half the sugar, a spoonful at a time, to make a stiff meringue. In a large bowl, beat the egg yolks with the rest of the sugar until pale and fluffy. Stir the melted chocolate mixture into the yolks, then fold in the whites.

Turn the batter into the baking dish and bake until the top is fully set across but the inside is still nice and gooey, about 15 minutes. (Do not over-bake, or you'll end up with a brownie, which is not the end of the world, but nor is it quite what you're after here.) Serve with crème fraîche and raspberries.

MAKES: 8 SERVINGS

Serve Yourself

I've written about this before, but I think the concept merits restating, because it is a most successful way of eliminating stress from hosting dinner parties. The secret is: buffet service. Now, stay with me for a moment. I know that "buffet" is a word that makes most of us cringe, conjuring up, as it does, chilling memories of all-you-can-eat-style restaurants where thousands of filthy hands have touched the same tongs and then thrown them back in on top of the salad before moving on to greedy scoops of this and that from a sea of chafing dishes. That's not, by "buffet service," at all what I'm suggesting, in terms of either service or food.

First of all, the food is obviously going to be the delicious meal you've so lovingly prepared: normal dinner. The difference, with this genius serving style, is that (a) you're not going to be stuck trying to plate each dish individually, thus making yourself a slave to the kitchen half the night, and (b) the delightful conversation around your table is not going to be interrupted constantly by people asking to have various heavy serving dishes passed—back and forth and up and down and across the table—to them.

No dining room requires a buffet proper to pull this off. You can just set up a narrow table at the end of the dining room (or dress up your kitchen counter a bit to serve the same purpose, depending on how you live). Then, you put all the elements of your main meal into serving dishes, set them on the buffet in a logical order, and let people file along and serve themselves.

I love this system for another reason: it allows people to control how much they take according to their tastes and appetite, rather than feel stuck with a dictatorially plated dish, which can often be intimidating. If anyone wants seconds, they can simply hop up and help themselves.

RASPBERRY CLAFOUTIS

This is the lightest clafoutis I've ever had. It's not a classic version, which I've always found too heavy and eggy for my liking anyway. The balance between the sweetness of the custard and the tartness of the berries is just right, and I adore the creaminess. Be sure to salvage the vanilla pod once you're through infusing the milk, so you can make vanilla sugar. And, of course, feel free to use pitted black cherries instead of raspberries, in the manner of *clafoutis original*.

1 cup (250 mL) heavy cream
1/2 vanilla bean, split lengthwise (or 1/2 teaspoon quality vanilla)
1/2 cup (95 g) sugar
1 egg
2 egg yolks
1 tablespoon flour
6 ounces (170 g) fresh raspberries
Icing sugar, for dusting

Heat the oven to 325°F (160°C). Pour the cream into a small saucepan, scrape the vanilla seeds into the cream, and add the pod. Bring just to a boil. Turn off the heat, cover, and leave to infuse for 10 minutes. (If you're using extract, heat the cream, stir in the vanilla, and carry right on without the infusion time.)

Meanwhile, in a medium bowl, beat the sugar, egg, egg yolks, and flour together until smooth. Tumble the raspberries into a 4-cup (1 L) baking dish. Remove the vanilla pod from the cream. Stirring constantly, add the cream to the egg mixture in a thin stream. Pour the custard over the berries.

Bake until set and golden on top, about 40 minutes. Cool to room temperature. Dust with icing sugar, and serve.

MAKES: 4 SERVINGS

ONE GIANT FINANCIER

Financiers generally come in the form of tiny rectangular cakes, requiring special moulds from France. This recipe, from a friend who rarely cooked (and *never* baked) until her children arrived, makes one big, luscious, almond-caramel financier that gets baked in a tart pan, which you probably own already and, if not, can buy anywhere. My friend buys caramel essence from the grocery store for scenting cakes, but if you can't find it, just stick to vanilla. The cake is nice alongside berries in summer. Or for a winter dinner, set out a bowl of clementines and a plate of walnut-stuffed dates to accompany it.

1 cup (125 g) ground almonds
1 cup (200 g) sugar
1/2 cup (60 g) flour
4 egg whites
2/3 cup (140 g) salted butter, melted
1/2 teaspoon vanilla or a few drops caramel essence
Icing sugar, for dusting

Heat the oven to 450°F (230°C). Grease a 12-inch (30 cm) tart pan with removable bottom. In a large bowl, stir together the almonds, sugar, and flour, then whisk in the egg whites until thoroughly combined. Whisk in the butter and vanilla.

Scrape the batter into the tart pan and bake until cooked through, about 15 minutes. Cool. Dust with icing sugar, and serve.

MAKES: 8 TO 10 SERVINGS

SPEEDY RUM BABA

This isn't a classic baba, because there is no yeast. However, despite the lack of yeasty taste, this does yield an impeccably textured rum-soaked cake that I can't get enough of. Serve with whipped cream, and pass the bottle o' rum for any bon vivant who'd relish an extra splash. For a crowd, double the cake and use an extra-large ring mould. It may take slightly longer to bake, but keep an eye on it and you'll have no troubles.

For the cake
1 cup (125 g) flour
1 teaspoon baking powder
4 eggs
1/2 cup + 2 tablespoons (125 g) sugar
1/2 teaspoon vanilla

For the syrup
1 cup (200 g) sugar
1-1/2 cups (375 mL) water
1/4 cup (60 mL) dark rum

Heat the oven to 350°F (180°C). Grease and flour a 9-inch (23 cm) savarin mould or other ring pan. (In a pinch, a loaf pan works, too.)

For the cake, sift together the flour and baking powder. In a large bowl, whisk the eggs, then beat in the sugar until thick and frothy. Stir in the vanilla, followed by the dry ingredients, to make a smooth batter. Pour into the baking pan. Bake until golden on top and a toothpick inserted in the centre comes out clean, about 40 minutes.

About 10 minutes before the cake comes out of the oven, make the syrup. Put the sugar and water in a saucepan. Bring to a boil and boil for 3 minutes. Remove from the heat and stir in the rum.

Turn the cake out onto a serving plate. Spoon the syrup slowly over the cake. It looks like a lot of syrup, but don't worry, the cake will absorb it all. Cool completely. Serve at room temperature with whipped cream.

MAKES: 8 SERVINGS

PICNIC CHOCOLATE CAKE

A friend once brought this rich and elegant cake to a picnic on the banks of the Seine, and served it rustically, straight from its terracotta baking dish. The world is knee deep in chocolate cake recipes, I know, but this has become one of my party staples, simplest made by following the metric measurements. I should warn you: it's more decadent than it sounds.

3/4 cup + 2 tablespoons (200 g) unsalted butter
7 ounces (200 g) dark chocolate
4 eggs
1 cup (200 g) sugar
1/4 cup (30 g) flour
1 lime or orange, for garnish

Heat the oven to 350°F (180°C). Grease and flour a 9-inch (23 cm) round cake pan (or terracotta tian, if you're in picnic mode).

In a medium heatproof bowl, gently melt the butter and chocolate over a pan of barely simmering water, stirring occasionally, until melted and smooth. Remove the bowl from the pan. Beat in the eggs, 1 at a time, followed by the sugar and flour. Pour into the cake pan. Bake until the top is just set and risen up, about 30 minutes. It won't look quite done, but the interior will firm up as the cake cools and shrinks and will have a wonderfully creamy texture. Finely grate some lime or orange zest over top before serving.

MAKES: 8 SERVINGS

COCONUT BREAD PUDDING

Gâteau de pain de la bonne Annette is how this recipe came to me, and although I never met Annette, I know she was on to something. This is a remarkably flexible recipe, and flavourings can be changed as you like (in which event, replace the coconut milk with half milk and half heavy cream). The extra yolk in the custard makes a creamier texture, but sticking to just 2 eggs also makes a fine pudding.

4 ounces (110 g) day-old baguette
1/2 cup (95 g) sugar
2 eggs
1 egg yolk
1/4 cup (55 g) butter, melted
1-1/2 cups (375 mL) well-shaken coconut milk
1/2 cup (125 mL) heavy cream
1 teaspoon vanilla
Zest of 1 lemon or lime
A handful or two of unsweetened shredded coconut

Heat the oven to 350°F (180°C). Butter a 4-cup (1 L) baking dish.

Cut the bread (or rip with your fingers) into tiny pieces. You'll finish up with about 2 cups (500 mL). Spread these in the baking dish. In a medium bowl, beat the sugar, eggs, and egg yolk until well blended, then whisk in the butter, coconut milk, cream, vanilla, and lemon zest. Pour over the crumbs. Scatter over the coconut.

Bake until the custard is set and the top is lightly golden, about 45 minutes. Cool to room temperature. Serve with slightly sweetened whipped cream.

MAKES: 6 SERVINGS

Pique-Nique

One friend in Paris is an expert picnic organizer. In fact, the first time I met him, he'd made a picnic instead of dinner and we ate it down on a rare grassy patch by the Seine. That was a simple picnic compared to what he normally does, which is to arrange large group picnics, often in the Arène de Lutèce, an old Roman arena in the 5th arrondissement. Everyone brings food and drink, which is laid out on cloths draped over the stone walls, and then, buffet style, we share. But there is a strict rule: no plastic, no paper. Each person brings his or her own cutlery, wineglass, and plate, and all of it must be the real thing. After all, the picnic organizer has dragged with him platters, cutting boards, wicker baskets of extra glasses, blankets... it's the least we can do to show respect. One time a newcomer showed up with the contribution of six boxes of take-out pizza. He was brutally scolded by everyone, although I do recall I, like the others, sneaked a piece of it myself.

LAZY BLACK FOREST YULE LOG

A proper French *bûche de Noël* is made with buttercream frosting, inside and out. It looks like a real log, and sometimes people garnish it with mushroom-shaped meringues for a full forest-floor effect. I've never really liked the look of those logs (too contrived?), and I'm not a great fan of over-doses of icing, either. So here is a Christmas log for the likes of me, one that is relatively light, less sweet, certainly quick to throw together, and every bit as festive as whatever you might consider "the real thing." It's a cream-filled kirsch-soaked chocolate roll cake served with sour cherries on the side. All a bit *Deutsch*, really, but then, it must be granted, the Germans are better at pulling off Christmas than the French any day. Note that the cake is best after sitting. If you're not a fan of kirsch, brush the cake with melted red currant jelly instead.

For the cake
6 tablespoons (45 g) sifted cake flour
6 tablespoons (45 g) cocoa powder
1/2 teaspoon baking powder
Pinch salt
4 eggs, separated
3/4 cup (155 g) sugar
1 teaspoon vanilla
Icing sugar, for dusting

For the filling and garnish
1 cup (250 mL) heavy cream
1/2 cup (125 mL) sour cream
1 tablespoon sugar, or to taste
2 to 3 tablespoons good-quality kirsch (optional)
1 pound (450 g) jarred sour cherries, drained (about 3 cups/750 mL)
Sifted cocoa powder, for dusting

Heat the oven to 400°F (200°C). Line a 15- × 10-inch (40 × 25 cm) jelly roll pan with parchment paper. Grease the parchment.

For the cake, sift together the flour, cocoa powder, baking powder, and salt. In a medium bowl, beat the egg yolks with 1/4 cup (55 g) of the sugar until thick and pale, then beat in the vanilla. In a very large bowl, beat the egg whites to soft peaks, then beat in the remaining 1/2 cup (100 g) sugar, a spoonful at a time, to achieve a stiff meringue. Fold a spoonful of the whites into the yolk mixture to loosen it, then pour the yolk mixture over the whites. Sift the dry ingredients over top and gently fold all together to combine thoroughly.

Pour the batter into the pan, spreading to the corners and smoothing to an even layer. Bake until the top springs back when pressed in the centre, about 12 minutes. Turn out onto a clean tea towel dusted with icing sugar. Peel off the parchment and roll (with the towel) lengthwise. Cool completely.

For the filling, in a large bowl, whip the cream, sour cream, and sugar to soft peaks.

To assemble the cake, unroll it. Brush the top with the kirsch (if using), then spread over the cream filling. If you like, you can scatter a few cherries right into the roll, but it's just as nice if you serve them all in a bowl on the side. Roll up the cake. Wrap in foil and refrigerate for several hours or overnight. Unwrap and transfer to a platter. Dust the top with sifted cocoa power just before taking it to the table with the bowl of cherries.

MAKES: 8 SERVINGS

Appliances

I have a few friends who are absolute appliance addicts (all of them men, as it happens). Whatever the latest gizmo is, they have to own it . . . and then they have to call me, bragging about all the things they can do with it. Yawn. Sorry, boys, but I just don't get it. An overabundance of clunky dust collectors taking up precious kitchen space, especially if you have a small kitchen, is a non-starter, so it's good to be wise about what one makes room for.

That said, and I swore it would never happen to me, but I have actually grown quite dependent on the food processor. I adore it for making pastry, bread crumbs, sauces, and purées, and it's marvellous for grinding leftover bits of roasted meat to make into stuffing or pies. If you get a simple model, they're not difficult to clean. (Mine is 20 years old, bought at the Salvation Army for a song.)

I also have an open mind about stand mixers because occasionally one does need that extra pair of hands. It will whisk the egg whites while you pour boiling syrup into them, for example. It will cream the butter and sugar and then, while you have a pot of melted chocolate in one hand and a spatula in the other, allow you to pour and scrape into the bowl without adorning a favourite white shirt with goo. An immersion blender is a godsend for speedy soups, although I find a proper blender does a better job when I want something super-smooth. Apart from that, there's really not a whole lot to dream of owning in the appliances department. A toaster oven, perhaps for nuts, and a kettle for endless cups of tea, but not much else. Because a key joy of cooking, especially these days, is being able to turn our backs on all that's automated in our lives and delve into the pleasures of messy hands.

FOOD PROCESSOR PROFITEROLES

Airy, adorable cream puffs are a breeze to make and a delight to everyone. To be classic, fill these with vanilla ice cream and drizzle with chocolate sauce. To be American, use whipped cream and berries for a variation on strawberry shortcake. To be romantic, top the puffs with sliced almonds before baking and serve them filled with sweetened, vanilla-flavoured whipped cream. You can always turn your back on dessert and take a savoury route, of course: just leave out the sugar and you're well on your way to a bite-sized French twist on lobster rolls for a drinks party.

1/3 cup (70 g) butter
1 tablespoon sugar
Pinch salt
1 cup (250 mL) water
1 cup (125 g) flour
4 eggs
Sliced almonds (optional)

Heat the oven to 375°F (190°C), using the convection setting if you plan to bake more than one tray at a time. Line 2 large baking sheets with parchment paper.

Put the butter, sugar, salt, and water in a roomy saucepan and bring to a boil. Remove from the heat and add the flour all at once, beating until it forms a ball and pulls away from the sides of the pan. Return the pan to the heat and continue beating so the dough dries out a little, about a minute.

Transfer the dough to a food processor. Whiz in 3 of the eggs, 1 at a time, processing thoroughly after each one. Whisk the last egg in a small bowl and add only as much of it as you need to achieve a smooth, thick, glossy paste. Whisk a teaspoon of water into the remaining egg and set aside for the glaze.

Spoon the dough into a piping bag and pipe 1-inch (2.5 cm) balls onto the baking sheets, leaving about 1/2 inch (1 cm) between balls. Dip your finger in cold water and gently pat down the tops. Brush with the glaze. Scatter almond slices over, if desired. Bake 1 sheet at a time (unless using the convection setting) until puffed, dry, and as light as Ping-Pong balls, 25 to 30 minutes.

Immediately slice each puff horizontally a third of the way from the top without cutting all the way through, so that the tops open like lids. Transfer to racks to cool completely. Store in an airtight container until serving. If they go a bit soft in storage, recrisp them in a 375°F (190°C) oven for 5 to 10 minutes.

To serve, fill with slightly sweetened vanilla-flavoured whipped cream.

MAKES: ABOUT 40 PUFFS

RED CURRANT CAKE

Tiny boxes of red currants are readily available at Paris greengrocers, and I always wondered what people did with them . . . until one day when I'd bought a few punnets and my dad called. "Have I got the cake for you!" he exclaimed. This one he'd just concocted, a rich, buttery cake that's beautiful to behold and has a perfect balance of tartness and sweetness. Thanks, Da!

1-1/2 cups (185 g) flour
2 teaspoons baking powder
1/4 teaspoon salt
1/2 cup (110 g) butter, softened
1 cup (200 g) sugar
2 eggs
1 teaspoon vanilla
3/4 cup (175 mL) milk
1-1/2 cups red currants (about 6 ounces/170 g)

Heat the oven to 350°F (180°C). Line the bottom of a 9-inch (23 cm) round cake pan with parchment paper.

Sift together the flour, baking powder, and salt. Set aside 2 tablespoons.

In a medium bowl, cream the butter with the sugar, then beat in the eggs and vanilla. Add the sifted ingredients alternately with the milk. Toss the currants with the reserved flour mixture to coat them, then stir them into the batter along with any remaining flour that slips off them.

Pour the batter into the cake pan and bake until the top is golden and a toothpick inserted into the centre comes out clean, 45 to 50 minutes. Run a knife around the edge of the cake. Cool completely on a rack before turning out onto a cake plate.

MAKES: 8 SERVINGS

All-Important Ambiance

It's baffling how many people decide that all the ambiance in a house belongs in the living room and that kitchens should be outfitted in the manner of dental clinics. The current thinking seems to be that if a kitchen is large and efficient, it should be a wonderful space to cook in, and yet so often these are precisely the kitchens that rarely produce so much as a cup of tea. I've learned from many a poor Parisian kitchen that personality can make up for a lot where practicality lacks, and it can be precisely the motivator needed for those who think they never have any inspiration to cook.

Parisian kitchens are notoriously small and cramped, the envy of no one. I've seen some with barely enough room for one person to turn around in, and yet they can be enchantingly alluring spaces, little nooks you just can't wait to stick your nose into, tiny workshops for the artistically inclined. And the meals that come out of some of them, and for crowds, too!

You'd think, with such small spaces, Parisians would take a minimalist approach to decor, but most don't. Indeed, most can't! There's rarely enough cupboard space for more than a few dishes, so inevitably pots and pans hang beckoning along the walls, knives stand at attention on a magnet above the only chopping space in the room, and jars of lentils, pasta, spices, and sugar elbow for space on the same shelves as coffee mugs and wineglasses.

As if this weren't enough, it's common for people to add to their mix a number of quirky touches that have no practical use whatsoever. Just when you think a Parisian has no room in the kitchen for so much as another toothpick, they'll suddenly uncover a narrow strip of precious shelf space ideal for parading their collection of hourglasses. An empty wall space might inspire another, and the next thing you know it's papered with wine labels or postcards. One friend's personal flourish even goes right out the window: the metal ledge on her sill is the perch for a flock of wooden bobbing-headed birds.

What is the point of all that? "Clutter," you want to cry! But it isn't clutter; it's comfort. It's delightful little bits of personality that remind you of who you are and make you comfortable and happy. Where you're comfortable and happy, you want to stay. And if you stay long enough, who knows, you might just start cooking.

BREAD BEIGNETS

I learned to make these magical bites in savoury form from a friend who spreads his beignets with rouille and serves them with clams (p. 59). Another friend, when I was showing her the recipe, decided to sprinkle them with sugar and nutmeg and then declared them to be better than doughnuts. These are cute, quick, and really quite astonishing. Put the coffee pot on!

1/2 loaf unsliced white bread, crusts removed

1 cup (250 mL) milk

2 eggs

Peanut oil, for frying

Sugar, for sprinkling

Nutmeg, for grating

Cut the bread into roughly 2-inch (5 cm) square chunks. Whisk together the milk and eggs in a bowl.

Heat about 1-1/2 inches (4 cm) oil in a saucepan over medium-high heat. The oil is ready when a rip of bread sizzles and starts to lightly colour. Dip a few pieces of bread in the milk mixture and lower into the oil. Fry, turning, until golden, about a minute. Remove to paper towels and immediately sprinkle with sugar and nutmeg. Continue with the remaining bread. Serve with coffee or a digestif.

MAKES: ABOUT 24 BEIGNETS

PEACH CRUMBLE

Fruit crumbles are extremely popular in France, where ground almonds take the place of oatmeal in the crumble topping. Obviously, peach is not the only way to go. Various fruits and berries work, so taste your filling and adjust the sugar to suit the fruit.

1/2 cup (60 g) flour
1/2 cup (70 g) ground almonds
1/4 cup (55 g) brown sugar
1/4 cup (55 g) butter, melted
1/4 teaspoon almond extract
Pinch cinnamon
2 pounds (900 g) peaches (about 4, depending on size)
About 2 tablespoons white sugar, to taste
1/2 cup (40 g) sliced almonds

Put the flour, ground almonds, brown sugar, butter, almond extract, and cinnamon in a bowl. Mix thoroughly with a fork. Refrigerate until crumble-able, about 30 minutes.

Heat the oven to 375°F (190°C). Butter a 12-inch (30 cm) tart pan or baking dish.

Bring a large pot of water to a boil. Score an X in the bottom of each peach, then plunge them into the water for 10 seconds. Drain and shock in ice-cold water. Peel, pit, and cut into wedges.

Toss the peaches with the white sugar and distribute evenly in the pan. Take the crumble from the fridge, break it up a bit with your fingers, and mix in the sliced almonds. Crumble evenly over the peaches.

Bake until the top is golden and the base bubbling, about 40 minutes. Serve warm or at room temperature.

MAKES: 6 TO 8 SERVINGS

SPECULOOS

I tend to make my sugar-topped lemon sablés (p. 277) look very feminine with a doily-edged cutter and pretty sugar garnish. But I give a more masculine edge to these light, crisp spice cookies by cutting them into rectangles and decorating them by merely poking a domino-like indentation in each of the four corners using the end of a chopstick. Very simple, but it looks great, like the detail on a good piece of tailoring.

1/2 cup (110 g) butter, softened
1 cup (200 g) brown sugar
1 egg
1 teaspoon vanilla
2 cups (250 g) flour
1 teaspoon baking powder
1 tablespoon ground ginger
2 teaspoons cinnamon
1/2 teaspoon nutmeg
1/4 teaspoon ground cloves

In a large bowl, cream the butter with the sugar. Beat in the egg and vanilla. Sift together the dry ingredients, add them to the butter mixture, and beat just until combined. Spill the dough onto plastic wrap, bundle it up, press into a brick, and refrigerate until firm enough to roll, about an hour.

Heat the oven to 375°F (190°C). Divide the dough in half for easy handling. Roll out 1 half on a lightly floured surface to 1/8- to 1/4-inch (3 to 5 mm) thickness. Cut with cookie cutters, or copy me and use a knife to cut into bar shapes. Decorate as you like, and arrange a batch on a baking sheet a finger-width apart. Bake until done, 8 to 10 minutes. Transfer to racks to cool completely. Continue with the remaining dough. Store in an airtight container.

MAKES: 40 TO 60 COOKIES, DEPENDING ON SIZE

A Social Breakfast

It sounds odd, I suppose, to invite people for breakfast, but then it's not unheard of for friends to meet in a café for their wake-up repast, so why not attempt the idea at home with close friends? I *have* seen it done, in Paris. Especially if you have a little activity you might partake in afterwards, such as a stomp in the park, or a visit to the Orangerie for an exhibit.

A Parisian breakfast is easy. All you need is a plunge pot of good coffee with warm milk in a pot on the side, then either bought croissants or "tartines" (baguette toasts).

The nicest tartines I think I've ever eaten were in a charmingly run-down café on rue Montcalm in Paris, which is nowhere near anything you've heard of. It is always filled with happy, joking locals of a certain age, dressed in a wardrobe you'd be tempted to write off as a cliché, except it's real. Anyway, at this place, café crème is served hot and in colourful cups with saucers, and with them come tartines made on *ficelles* rather than baguette (ficelles being a thinner version of basically the same). Leave it to Parisians to make even a piece of toast look chic! For their tartines, each ficelle is first cut in half crosswise, then sliced lengthwise through the centre, so you get four kayaks of bread. Along they come with cold butter, which looks as though it was applied by a bricklayer, and finally sweet silky swaths of apricot jam.

I never think more than that is needed on offer for breakfast, but if, at home, you have a fruit eater on your hands, I can recommend half a papaya, seeded and squirted with lime; or half a grapefruit, the sections already separated for them and sugar on hand for wimps; or a mango porcupine, which is simply mango cheeks in their skins, scored into cubes, then turned inside out and laid in a juicy hump on a plate. One Paris friend always has heaps of kiwi fruit on offer, which I initially found hilariously 1980s, but now I've decided is "cool," so I'm going to copy it.

SUGAR-TOPPED LEMON SABLÉS

These light, crisp, lemony biscuits whip up quickly, roll like a dream, and taste great with tea or alongside creamy or fruit desserts. Feel free to use almond or lemon extract in place of vanilla. And switch up the toppings to suit your mood, too. I've poked in a pecan, or a few slivers of almond, occasionally a pistachio—just a little something to dress them up. I've also chucked handfuls of chopped nuts right into the batter for nut cookies. If you'd like a glazed look (I often have a glazed look myself . . .), simply brush the tops with egg wash (an egg beaten with a teaspoon of water) before baking.

3/4 cup (140 g) butter, softened
3/4 cup (155 g) sugar
1 egg
1/2 teaspoon vanilla
Zest of 2 lemons
2 cups (250 g) flour
Coarse sugar, for garnish

Cream the butter with the sugar. Beat in the egg, vanilla, and lemon zest. Finally beat in the flour just until combined. Wrap the dough in plastic and refrigerate until firm enough to roll, about an hour.

Heat the oven to 350°F (180°C). Divide the dough in half. On a lightly floured surface, roll out 1 piece of dough to 1/8- to 1/4-inch (3 to 5 mm) thickness. Using a 2-inch (5 cm) round cookie cutter, cut out cookies. Arrange about 15 cookies on a baking sheet and sprinkle a bit of coarse sugar onto the centre of each; press lightly so it sticks. Bake until the cookies are just getting golden at the edges, 8 to 10 minutes. Transfer to racks to cool. Repeat with remaining dough. Store in an airtight container.

MAKES: ABOUT 45 (2-INCH/5 CM) COOKIES

WALNUT CUSTARD TART
for the PASTRY-PHOBIC

Blitz the pastry ingredients to crumbs and press them into your tart pan and that's as complicated as this pastry gets. Filled with walnuts and custard, this is a fine tart for an autumn day, to serve with afternoon tea or for dessert following a warming, stewy dinner. I like it when the walnuts sort of float into their own positions, but if you want them to stay where you put them, press them into the pastry base before refrigerating. That way, when you pour over the custard, they won't move.

For the pastry
1 cup (125 g) flour
1/3 cup (70 g) butter, cut into pieces
1 tablespoon icing sugar
1 teaspoon vanilla

For the filling
2 eggs + 1 egg yolk (or 3 eggs)
1/3 cup (70 g) brown or white sugar
1 teaspoon vanilla
1 cup (250 mL) heavy cream
3/4 cup (100 g) walnut halves

Heat the oven to 350°F (180°C). For the pastry, put all the ingredients into a food processor, pulse to fine crumbs, and spill into a 9-inch (23 cm) tart pan with removable bottom. Spread them out evenly and press with your fingers to line the bottom and sides with a crust. Refrigerate for 15 minutes.

For the filling, beat the eggs and sugar together with a fork, then beat in the vanilla, followed by the cream.

Arrange the walnut halves over the tart base, then pour over the custard. Bake until the custard is puffed up, golden on top, and set in the middle, 40 to 45 minutes. Cool completely. Serve at room temperature or even slightly chilled.

MAKES: 8 SERVINGS

CHERRY ALMOND PUFF PASTRY TART

This is a pretty, seasonal tart that you can throw together on a baking sheet in no time. It adorns a table beautifully, and it's great fun to eat with your hands.

1/2 cup (70 g) ground almonds
1/4 cup (55 g) unsalted butter
1/4 cup (55 g) sugar
2 tablespoons flour
1 egg yolk
A few drops of almond extract
1 all-butter puff pastry sheet (10 inches/25 cm square), thawed if frozen
2 cups (375 g) halved pitted cherries

Heat the oven to 375°F (190°C). Put the almonds, butter, sugar, and flour in a food processor and pulse until a paste forms. Add the egg yolk and almond extract; pulse just until combined.

Leaving the pastry on its parchment, roll it in a single direction to extend it to a rectangle, roughly 13 × 10 inches (33 × 25 cm). Slide it, on its parchment, onto a baking sheet. Prick the pastry all over with a fork. Spread over the nut paste, leaving a 3/4-inch (2 cm) border around the edges. Scatter the cherries evenly over the top. Fold over and pinch the border to make an edge.

Bake until the pastry is puffed and golden, about 30 minutes. Serve at room temperature.

MAKES: 8 SERVINGS

Fruit Tarts Galore

Fruit tarts are practically a national obsession in France. No wonder, since they are one of the easiest and most delicious desserts to make—and are not unhealthy either. Any fruit you have around will do, whether it be fresh and ripe or already cooked.

Here's an easy formula for a buttery pastry that's good for any fruit tart: Put 1-1/4 cups (155 g) flour with 6 tablespoons (50 g) icing sugar in a food processor, then drop in 1/2 cup (110 g) butter, cut into pieces. Pulse to crumbs. Then, add two egg yolks and 1/2 teaspoon vanilla and pulse again just until the dough comes together, a matter of seconds. Spill the dough onto a piece of plastic wrap, pat into a disk, wrap, and refrigerate an hour to rest. (Yield: between 8 and 12 small tarts.)

Now, exactly how you bake the dough depends on what sort of fruit you're using in your tart(s). If you have very ripe, fresh berries or already-poached stone fruit, such as apricots or peaches, then you'll want to bake the pastry on its own first. The simplest thing is to make "cookie" pastry bases, which means rolling the dough about 1/4-inch (60 mm) thick and cutting it into, say, 4-inch (10 cm) rounds—or, go crazy and do rectangles—before baking them at 350°F (180°C) on a cookie sheet until done, about 10 minutes. Once cool, brush the tops with melted apricot jam or red currant jelly and arrange berries on top, or simply pile on poached fruit and serve with whipped cream. To blind bake proper tart shells, line the shell(s) with pastry, then with parchment, before filling to the brim with dried beans and baking 10 minutes to set the dough. Once it's secure, remove the beans and parchment and continue baking until the base is lightly golden, 10 to 15 minutes longer for a 9- to 12-inch (23 to 30 cm) tart shell, slightly less time for smaller tarts. Once cool, the fresh or poached fruit goes on top.

If, alternatively, you have uncooked fruit at your disposal, such as apples or pears—or even overripe berries that need salvaging—forget about blind baking and put the fruit, tossed with a bit of sugar, directly onto raw-pastry-lined tart shells. (You could also lay the fruit on raw "cookie tart" bases in a thin layer.) Bake until the fruit is tender and the pastry crisp, about 30 minutes, depending on the fruit.

You see, no need for a thousand different recipes!

APPLE TART
with SUGARED WALNUTS
and ROSEMARY SYRUP

Tarte fine aux pommes is a thin apple tart, in this instance on puff pastry. I love how extremely light it is and how, with the sugared walnuts and rosemary, it walks just barely on the sweet side of the border across from savoury land. (Peaches are good here, too.) The tart can be made ahead and reheated to serve, but save the syrup step until just before serving. Be sure to buy good-quality puff pastry made of butter. What other potholes . . . hmm . . . Oh yes, if you pile on too much fruit, the pastry won't crispen properly, so keep yourself in check.

For the tart

1 all-butter puff pastry sheet (10 inches/25 cm square), thawed if frozen

3 to 4 Granny Smith apples

1/4 cup (55 g) sugar, more or less, depending on tartness of apples

2 tablespoons butter, melted

1/2 cup (60 g) walnuts, coarsely chopped

A small handful of fresh rosemary leaves

For the syrup

1/4 cup (60 mL) water

2 tablespoons sugar

Juice of 1 lemon

1 teaspoon finely chopped fresh rosemary

Heat the oven to 375°F (190°C). Leaving the pastry on its parchment, roll it in a single direction to extend it to a rectangle, roughly 13 × 10 inches (33 × 25 cm). Slide it on its parchment onto a baking sheet.

Peel the apples. Cutting close to the core, cut the cheeks off the apples on either side, then cut off the remaining sides. Discard the core. Lay the apple bits core side down and slice thinly. Toss with 3 tablespoons of the sugar and half of the butter. Take a bite of apple, and add a little more sugar if necessary. Arrange the apple slices in a single overlapping layer over the pastry, going right to the edges. Toss the walnuts with the remaining sugar and butter and scatter over the apples. Bake until the pastry is golden, the apples are soft, and the walnuts are caramelized, about 30 minutes.

While the tart bakes, make the syrup. Put all the ingredients in a saucepan and boil until the syrup lightly coats the back of a spoon, about 15 minutes.

Remove the tart from the oven and brush the apples with the syrup. Scatter over the rosemary leaves, and serve.

MAKES: 4 TO 6 SERVINGS

Weight a Minute!

When I first lived in Europe, in my early twenties, I remember the dread of trying to cook from European recipes. My first experience was in Germany, where of course baking is a national sport and where I have no doubt the modern weighing machine was perfected, if not invented. For dry ingredients, measuring cups are simply not used. Kitchen scales are the norm.

I remember having it argued to me in the beginning why scales were so much easier. I didn't buy it. Of course, 20 years on and fully converted, I'm now as evangelical as they come. Scales are easier, and much more accurate, for many ingredients, particularly flour. Scales also require less cleaning up: often you can use one bowl on scales rather than four or five measuring cups and spoons.

Measuring cups have their merits—for liquids, obviously—and I use them as well, but I cannot fathom a kitchen without scales. If you've never tried cooking with scales, I urge you to give it a go. It's not a difficult language to learn, and once you have it down you can navigate cookbooks from many different countries with ease.

A HARD DAY'S NIGHT
HOT CHOCOLATE

I'm not a dessert eater unless I've invited guests—in other words, usually only on weekends. However, there are Wednesdays known to stretch patience to the snapping point, not to mention insomnia, and various other workaday states of emergency. All of these can be soothed, at least to some extent, by a mug of Cognac-spiked cocoa. A very useful back-pocket recipe for relaxation.

1 cup (250 mL) whole milk
1 tablespoon cocoa powder
1 to 2 tablespoons sugar
1 tablespoon Cognac, more to taste

Heat the milk gently in a saucepan. Put the cocoa powder, sugar, and Cognac in a mug and stir to make a paste. Gradually add the hot milk, stirring. Taste, adding more Cognac if you're desperate.

MAKES: 1 SERVING

Hark, I Hear . . . Dinner

I'm not sure when it first struck me—probably it has struck me more than once over the years—but dinner in Paris actually has a sound, like music. I'm not being romantic; I'm serious. If you wander the streets any time between, say, 8 and 11 at night, any season of the year, you'll hear what I mean. At first you don't notice because you're walking and you have a destination and your thoughts are very loud after a long, hard day. Then you become aware of your own footsteps and you realize, with a bit of a start, how amazingly quiet the city can be. It may take you months before you realize that one of the reasons it's so quiet is that Paris shops and restaurants don't blast music out their doors. (If a restaurant has music on, it's because there's nobody in there yet and they're trying to lure; as people start filling the tables, the music will be turned down and down again until it's finally turned off, exactly the opposite of how things work in North America, where by the time you've got to your main coarse you've gone deaf and hoarse and have given up entirely on trying to converse with your dining companion.) At last (we're back in peaceful Paris now), because your mind has quieted down enough, you hear the "music" . . . As you wander the snakes and ladders of streets, it comes to you on the air: the percussive clinking of cutlery and glasses, the singsong orders being called out in cafés, the murmur of thousands of people talking to each other, laughing, arguing, flirting, complaining, revelling, tête-à-tête. It must be one of the most marvellous sounds in the world, and it goes on for hours. It's a sound I've only ever heard in Paris.

CAFE
RESTAURAN
LE CEPA

APPRECIATION

My life in Paris is largely lived in expat circles, which, perhaps contrary to popular belief, doesn't make it any less Parisian. Sometimes I think it makes it more so. I'm not suggesting Parisians take what they have for granted, but those of us who have been drawn to the city for all its charms can sometimes be so starved for them by the time we get there that we often try even harder to indulge ourselves to the full, to live lives more Parisian than those born and bred in the place. Many of the recipes in this book come from this crowd and those affiliated. I'd like to thank these friends, and a few others, for so generously sharing their own culinary discoveries and inventions with me. They are:

Christopher Mooney, Kevin Mooney, Geoffrey Finch, Kasper Winding, Ancuța Iordăchescu, Claes Hanson, Odette Kruger, John Calder, David Jaggard, Barbara Goraczko, Betsy Bernardaud, Rebeca Plantier, Graham Pratt, Mark and Judith Phillips, Pam Duffin, Roseline Leyuraz Fallecker, Philip Haddad, John Evans, Oliver Evans, Tina Isaac, Patricia Hawkes, Tony Suche, Ann Godin, Cathy Grant, Patti Hetherington, Ivan Simmonds, Nathalie Findlay, Nancy Sherry, Trine Miller, Eylem Rodriguez, Camille Labro, and Dan Hayes.

Writing a book of any sort is, at several stages, a solitary activity, but no book ever sees the light of day without the strong support of a team. I thank my long-time editor and friend, Kirsten Hanson, at HarperCollins Canada, for her ongoing encouragement and enthusiasm, as well as copy editor Shaun Oakey. I thank my literary agent, Grainne Fox, at Fletcher and Company in New York City, for her adept handling of business affairs. Thanks to Patti Hetherington for her delectable food styling (and for flying to Paris for the job), to Ancuţa Iordăchescu for her photography of food and scenes of Paris, and to Mark Hemmings for photographing the cover. Thanks to everyone at HarperCollins Canada, from the legal department to publicity, for their hard work, and especially to Lisa Bettencourt for the beautiful design of this book and to Alan Jones for the inspired cover. Finally, thanks to all my family and friends for being such reliable recipe testers and taste testers throughout the process, and especially to my mother, Doris Calder, who went through the text with a fine-tooth comb before my final submission.

INDEX